Here We Go Again...

Here We Go Again...

UNPUBLISHED LETTERS

TO

The Daily Telegraph

EDITED BY KATE MOORE

Aurum

Brimming with creative inspiration, how-to projects, and useful information to enrich your everyday life, quarto.com is a favourite destination for those pursuing their interests and passions.

First published in 2022 by Aurum,
an imprint of The Quarto Group
One Triptych Place,
London, SE1 9SH, United Kingdom

www.Quarto.com/Aurum

ISBN: 978-0-7112-7763-2
Ebook ISBN: 978-0-7112-7764-9

10 9 8 7 6 5 4 3 2 1

2026 2025 2024 2023 2022

Typeset in Mrs Eaves by SX Composing DTP, Rayleigh, Essex

Printed and bound by CPI Group (UK) Ltd, Croydon, CR0 4YY

Jacket Design by Darren Jordan

CONTENTS

INTRODUCTION

Crisis? Which crisis?

Anyone writing to a newspaper in 2022 needed to be specific. So much happened, and kept on happening, that even the shrewdest observers might have struggled to keep up. The first four months alone saw mass protests in Canada, spiking Covid-19 cases, the Russian invasion of Ukraine, fuel shortages, Storm Malik and Storm Eunice. By the summer, inflation and tempers were rising with alarming speed. With much of the public sector in disarray, the British people took in refugees, battled on through strikes and baked under a heatwave. In Westminster, an array of scandals (most of them ending in "-gate") threw the Government into chaos and unseated Boris Johnson. Wherever one looked, something seemed to be falling apart.

In their letters to the editor, *Telegraph* readers prevailed on Larry the Downing Street cat to intervene. Others began constructing their own fantasy Cabinets to restore harmony, perhaps drawn from the Common Sense Group of Conservative MPs or – better still – the cast of *The Repair Shop*. Everyone, regardless of background or political affiliation, became sick of the word *unprecedented*. Regrettably, no other word would do.

There were lighter moments, if you looked hard enough. The "Wagatha Christie" libel battle kept headline writers and lovers of soap opera happy for months. The Winter Olympics briefly turned everyone into curling fans, and Glastonbury went ahead for the first time since 2019. The nation came together to mark 70 years under Queen Elizabeth, with knitted corgis and Union flags in abundance. Paddington Bear had a leading role in the celebrations, his antics doing much for the reputation of marmalade.

But in good times and grim, the *Telegraph*'s letter-writers have carried the day. Whatever the subject, they have responded with acuity, opening up ever more avenues for debate. Why, someone wonders, can't Vladimir Putin emulate another megalomaniac and retire to play billiards on St Helena? Can a prime minister really be "ambushed by a cake"? And what happens to coronavirus variants after we polish off the Greek alphabet?

We on the Letters Desk have benefitted from all manner of insights. One reader finds a parallel between the Tory leadership candidates and the Gloster canaries that he once bred for show (it's all in the hair). There is wry recognition for Neil Parish MP, who got into trouble "looking for tractors". Nicola Sturgeon, the England men's cricket team, Sir Tony Blair, Will Smith, Chris Pincher and Raphael Nadal's underpants have all come under scrutiny. Few, if any, have emerged unscathed.

Naturally, there is life beyond the headlines. Within this volume you will discover *Telegraph* readers' thoughts on everything from sex to gardening; the aesthetic benefits of masks and the delight of an encounter with one's GP; the trials of getting fit, getting older, getting sober (or getting drunk); the battle to stop nouns becoming verbs and chairmen from becoming items of furniture; the struggle to kick a serious Wordle habit, and the perils of being improperly dressed for a food fight at a formal dinner. In a tumultuous year, the letter-writers have maintained their good humour and – best of all – their delightful eccentricity. I hope you will enjoy their company as much as I have.

As ever, I must thank all our correspondents and my colleagues on the Letters Desk – in particular the Letters Editor, Christopher Howse. Thanks also go to Rachel Welsh for casting her legal eye over everything; to Matt for his cover illustration; to Katie Bond, Jennifer Barr and all the good people at Aurum, and to Melissa Smith for her wisdom and guidance in the crucial final stages.

Here we go again...

Kate Moore
London SW1

FAMILY
TRIALS AND
TRIBULATIONS

Is anybody there?

SIR – The message from call centres appears to be: Your call is important to us; please continue to hold until it is no longer important to you.

Nick Jones
Cardiff

SIR – In future, callers to my number may be told that I am unable to come to the phone right now as I am experiencing an unusually high volume of things to do.

David Fishwick
Wallington, Surrey

SIR – Should BT Openreach be renamed BT Outofreach?

June Green
Bagshot, Surrey

SIR – I asked my daughter to brush her teeth. She replied: "I'll think about it. I'll get back to you in three to four working days."

Mark Solon
London E1

SIR – Although I am retired I am happy for my name to be put forward for a "job" at the DVLA. As I understand it, I can stay at home, get paid a full salary and will not get "disturbed" by my boss. Should

I get chosen I will speak with my wife to see if she is also available for work.

Idris White
Sevenoaks, Kent

SIR – In the early days of working from home, my wife, on the phone to Sainsbury's, complained about the background noise.

"Oh," said the man, "that's my brother cooking his dinner."

Roy Miller
Wakefield, West Yorkshire

SIR – Perhaps the enthusiasm for "working from home" would be reduced if it was renamed "living at work".

Perception is key.

Guy Bargery
Edinburgh

SIR – With apologies to William Wordsworth:

For oft, when on my couch I lie
In vacant or in pensive mood.
When wicked Wordles pass me by
And daytime telly has been viewed,
No daffodil tempts me to roam.
'Tis better far to work from home!

Penny Dorritt
Walmer, Kent

Locked down and fed up

SIR – According to the Mental Health Foundation and Independent Age, coronavirus restrictions have caused over-65s to suffer from negative emotions such as loneliness, despair, fear and grief. They forgot blind incoherent rage.

Philippa Lloyd
London SE17

SIR – This morning I received a text message from NHS Test & Trace informing me that I had been in contact with someone with the Omicron variant.

This was astounding news as I have been in Doha, Qatar since January and had absolutely no appreciation of the global reach and coverage of our world-beating Test & Trace system. That was £37 billion well spent.

Trelawney Ffrench
Doha, Qatar

SIR – Yesterday, towards the end of a week-long river cruise in France, I learnt that I had tested positive for Covid. I now face isolation for seven days in a Bordeaux hotel.

I had no symptoms before the test and to date I have not experienced any of the common after-effects. However, for the first time in my 72 years, I woke up last night with the urge to write pandemic poetry.

Have any other readers experienced this? Is there a cure? And can anyone help with a word that rhymes with JVT?

Brian Duckworth
Hucknall, Nottinghamshire
(but temporarily in Bordeaux)

SIR – If, as reported, the going rate for administering a booster Covid-19 jab is going to be £15 with a bonus for working at the weekend, I would like to volunteer my services. There is one caveat: of the 40,000 or so jabs that I have administered, only about six have been to another person (my late wife). I am a Type 1 Diabetic.

Philip Barry
Dover, Kent

SIR – Back in the 1950s children queued happily for vaccinations and the school nurse rewarded us with a chocolate button. To encourage modern adults to get jabbed for Covid, perhaps liqueur chocolates might be used to entice them.

John Pritchard
Ingatestone, Essex

Time to face the world

SIR – Having popped out this morning for my Saturday *Telegraph*, I was reminded by the lovely young man in the shop that it was no longer necessary to wear a mask. I replied that my mask was nothing to do with safety, more to hide the fact that I had forgotten to put my false tooth in. He went off chuckling.

> **Mary Gorman**
> Warrington, Cheshire

SIR – My wife feels that there are certain benefits on the occasions when I wear a mask. She tells me that I don't frighten as many children.

> **Jack Crawford**
> Dorridge, Warwickshire

SIR – Can we please bring back compulsory masks on trains? It was much nicer for everyone not to see me sleeping with my mouth open.

> **Lynda Cox**
> Southampton

SIR – A mask and behind-the-ear hearing aids are incompatible. If you wear them, never remove your mask near a drain.

> **Philip Corp**
> Salisbury, Wiltshire

SIR – The mandatory use of masks delighted me as it was a deterrent to unsolicited lips. It is my fervent wish that the excessive osculatory continental habit be put behind us. Kissing should be for one's wife and then reserved for memorable occasions such as silver and gold wedding anniversaries.

Dr Robert J. Leeming
Coventry, Warwickshire

SIR – I will wear a mask in Tesco etc. if asked to do so by someone whose medical qualifications are at least the equivalent of mine.

David Nunn MB BS LRCP FRCS Eng, Ed, Orth
West Malling, Kent

The doctor won't see you now

SIR – While browsing TV channels the other day I came across a programme entitled GPs: Behind Closed Doors. I thought it was strange to make a programme about the bleeding obvious.

Andy Hodsman
Somerton, Somerset

SIR – This morning I booked a vet appointment for my dog and was offered a consultation later today. Such a rapid response from my GP service would be more than welcome – although I would happily forgo the biscuit and ear ruffle.

Graeme Williams
West Malling, Kent

SIR – In the time it took to hear the recorded message relating Covid-19 restrictions at my local GP's surgery, I managed to put on a wash, empty the dishwasher, feed the birds, read this morning's front page and load my car with tools for today's work.

Kate Peeters
Kingsbridge, Devon

SIR – I find it hard to understand why so many of your letter-writers find it so difficult to see their GP. A friend of mine has seen his own GP twice in the last two days, once in Marks & Spencer and once in Waitrose.

Colin Eldred
Eastbourne, East Sussex

SIR – Following a routine blood test, my GP considered it necessary to conduct a physical examination of my prostate. As it was not practical to conduct this procedure remotely I was asked to attend the surgery.

It is fair to say that the consultation was person to person, but not exactly face to face.

Michael Price
Ashford, Surrey

SIR – Dr Nick Watts, the Chief Sustainability Officer for the NHS, points out that not having to travel to GP surgeries for face-to-face consultations has led to a reduction in carbon emissions.

Next week perhaps he will point out that being unable to access medical help has caused many people to stop breathing, reducing carbon emissions even further.

Ray Cantrell
Colchester, Essex

SIR – Serious consideration should be given to the imposition of hefty fines on those patients who have the impertinence to fall sick at night and weekends. This would help to reduce the need for GPs to work inconvenient hours while adding to the coffers for their substantial pay rises.

David Taylor
Dersingham, Norfolk

SIR – Perhaps visits to hospitals could be reduced by sending DIY kits to patients with clear instructions on how to carry out operations (in large print for the elderly). Hip or knee operations may prove a bit of a challenge but with the help of a friendly neighbour they may be doable.

D. Hinton
Chichester, West Sussex

SIR – I felt that I needed a doctor's appointment recently. The receptionist at the surgery was unhelpful until I asked her: "Can you recommend a good local undertaker?"

I received my appointment.

Peter Vince
Horsted Keynes, West Sussex

SIR – The allocation of just a few minutes per patient per GP consultation makes it very hard to achieve an accurate diagnosis. I remember an occasion when the patient produced a referral letter from his GP which was very brief. It read: "? Heart."

The accurate reply read: "Yes one".

Dr Rhoda Pippen
Cardiff

Theatre of the absurd

SIR – During my recent operation the theatre muzak included "Killing Me Softly". What would be more appropriate – "Mack the Knife", perhaps?

Tom Wilson
Edinburgh

SIR – The cardiologist who inserted stents after my husband's heart attack spoke to me after the procedure. He had discovered some coronary artery variant and asked me if I was aware that my husband was "very unusual anatomically". I replied that after 30 years of marriage there were no surprises left.

Janet Rennison
Bowdon, Cheshire

SIR – We were holding our weekly meeting today and during the symptoms, treatments and remedies section, one party indicated that he would be missing next week as he was undergoing an autopsy at the local hospital. It transpired to be a biopsy but we all agreed that, either way, he ought to be there.

John Stuart Dunn
Rhos-on-Sea, Colwyn Bay

SIR – In preparation for an MRI scan next month, I have been asked a number of questions in advance including question number 9: are you pregnant? This is preposterous as I was born during the war so am clearly beyond child-bearing age.

Jeremy Burton
Wokingham, Berkshire

SIR – When I was "awarded" my pension just over a year ago, I had to chuckle when the nice lady from the Department for Work and Pensions asked me if I was pregnant. I laughed even more when she recounted that another gentleman had replied when asked his marital status that he was a widower – and she then heard a booming but unmistakably female voice in the background shout, "Not bloody yet you're not!"

John May
Arkesden, Essex

In tip-top shape

SIR – I note that, for good health, my waist measurement should be less than half my height.
Clearly I'm simply not tall enough.

Joe Greaves
Fleckney, Leicestershire

SIR – There is emerging evidence that, since the Industrial Revolution, a more sedentary lifestyle has led to a modern prevalence of back problems.
Is it possible, then, that Monty Python's Spanish In-quisition actually knew what they were doing with the call to "fetch the comfy chair"?

Charles Smith-Jones
Landrake, Cornwall

SIR – As an experiment, I decided to march around my sitting room in time with the 1st Battalion Irish Guards at Trooping the Colour on 2 June. I have inadvertently discovered a new fitness regime as I now march to the shops.

Jane Moth
Stone, Staffordshire

SIR – I lose count of the number of times I walk through the house to locate something that is staring my husband in the face. It all adds up to a very healthy, if exasperating, daily step count.

Lesley Thompson
Lavenham, Suffolk

SIR – Now that we have endured Stoptober, Movember and Veganuary, I suggest we all give blood in Phlebruary.

Roger Willatt
Lyndhurst, Hampshire

SIR – I gave up smoking aged about 10, in 1960, when I bought a pack of five Woodbines, a penny box of matches and a packet of Polos, so that my mother couldn't smell smoke on my breath.

All children should be encouraged to smoke when they are very young; it'll put them off it for life.

Rob Dorrell
Bath, Somerset

I'll drink to that

SIR – Somewhat surprisingly, my local pub supported Dry January. The billboard said: "During January we will be serving dry martinis, dry cider and dry white wine."

Sandy Pratt
Storrington, West Sussex

SIR – A pub I used to frequent sold only three types of crisps: plain, ready salted and potato flavoured.

Robin Lane
Devizes, Wiltshire

SIR – Thank you for your excellent and persuasive article recommending a Sober September. I'll start on the 29th.

Dave Alsop
Churchdown, Gloucestershire

SIR – My doctor has given me three days to give up drinking. In order to comply, I've chosen 27 June, 28 July and 10 October.

Peter Burgess
Eastbourne, East Sussex

SIR – The definition of a "big" drinker has always been very simple. It is someone who drinks more than his doctor.

Dr P. J. Irvin
Nunthorpe, North Yorkshire

SIR – When we lived in Crawley for two years
between 2013 and 2015, we were most impressed
to discover shops at Victoria Station selling wine in
sealed plastic goblets specially designed for the train.
We loved British trains anyway; this just made them
even better.

> **Valerie O'Neill**
> East Perth, Australia

SIR – You report that half of those studied by the
University of Cambridge were unable to tell when
they were too drunk to drive.

I look forward to the university's upcoming
magnum opus on whether or not animals in the
order Ursa actually defecate in forests.

> **Simon Crowley**
> Kemsing, Kent

SIR – Several years ago, following a Christmas party in
the Officers' Mess and suffering appropriately, I was
advised by a senior that hair of the dog is the only
surefire antidote:

"The first will hurt; the second will nearly kill you
but, if you can make it the third, you'll be alright."

> **Matt Walter**
> Ashford, Surrey

SIR – When I was a newly qualified pharmacist
the hospital pharmacy had a "drinks cabinet".
Sherry, lager, whisky and brandy were dispensed on
prescription. The brandy was largely to help panicking
relatives, or about-to-be fathers.

Margaret Baker
Juvigny Les Vallées, Manche, France

SIR – My aunt Eileen in Cork always had a bottle of
Guinness included in her weekly groceries "for the
weakness".

Bill Nimmo-Scott
Pewsey, Wiltshire

SIR – The Scottish National Party's efforts to curb
problem drinking are now deemed to have failed.

Years ago a friend took a bottle of gin to the till
desk of an Edinburgh corner shop on a Sunday.
The shopkeeper said, "I am sorry, sir. I cannot sell it
to you legally."

He replied, "That's alright, I'll buy it illegally."

"Thank you very much. That will be £6.99."

Donald MacKenzie
Inverness

SIR – When my wife and I checked into our holiday
hotel in Scotland after travelling from London,
I asked the waiter for a large Johnnie Walker with
some ice.

He returned bearing a large jug of water and a bowl of ice cubes.

From then on I simply asked for a Scotch on the rocks.

Robert Danny
West Molesey, Surrey

Kitchen nightmares

SIR – I am accused of messy marmalade-making by my wife on account of the multiple times I have let the mix boil all over the Aga. When asked for the recipe by a friend I told him that the first thing to do was make up a bed in the spare room.

George Bastin
Stroud, Gloucestershire

SIR – My younger son must have had some reservations about our home cooking: aged four or five he was told by my wife that if he didn't behave himself he would be sent to his room and have no supper. He deliberated for a moment before replying, "What's for supper?"

Peter Fineman
Mere, Wiltshire

SIR – When my father retired from the Army, never having cooked anything other than compo during his military career, he was given the task of Sunday night supper.

Sometimes delicious, sometimes questionable, it was always known as compost soup.

Cilla Mayne
Romsey, Hampshire

SIR – At school we had "Jesus Christ soup": the same yesterday, today and forever.

Rev Roger Holmes
Howden, East Yorkshire

SIR – On the rare occasions that my mother was ill enough to stay in bed my stepfather would take over in the kitchen. There would be much commotion and finally his naval speciality, bubbliato, would be produced.

The recipe was fairly flexible, as I remember it. The contents of the fridge was tipped into a great deal of bubbling oil with onion and garlic. Then it was fried ferociously.

Bubbliato evolved over the days. It permeated the entire house. It lingered.

My mother made astonishingly quick recoveries due to bubbliato.

Sue Gordon
Sandwich, Kent

SIR — I was fascinated to read an article in *The Daily Telegraph* today about a scientific study proving that keeping fruit and veg in the fridge makes them last longer.

Previously I was keeping mine in the warming oven of the Aga. I wondered why they were going off so fast.

Dr Philip M. Peverley
Sunderland, Co Durham

SIR — According to your report, cucumbers will get the chop when farmers see increased heating bills resulting from the current energy crisis. At last, something positive has come out of this unhappy situation: the demise of a vegetable that is totally lacking in both taste and nutritional value.

Barri N. Stirrup
Kilby, Leicestershire

Live and let diet

SIR — I recently received an invitation to join a bell-ringing course which includes lunch. The application form kindly asks whether I am vegetarian, vegan or celeriac.

Lesley Walford
Pewsey, Wiltshire

SIR — Scientists have now shown that quitting steaks and sausages by the age of 60 would add 10 years to our lives. The pity, as pointed out by the comedian Jack Dee, is they'll be the last 10 years.

Dr David Slawson
Nairn, Inverness-shire

SIR — Every winter my father would regularly make cheese and raw onion sandwiches for my brother and me. I think we were kept free of winter bugs thanks to our lack of friends, rather than the efficacy of the raw onion.

Sandra Knatchbull
Maidstone, Kent

SIR — I've learnt in the last few days that a hot dog will reduce my life expectancy by 30 minutes, while a peanut butter and jam sandwich will extend it by the same margin.

This appears to be the perfectly balanced diet at last.

Denis Kearney
Lostwithiel, Cornwall

SIR — School breakfasts with marmalade on fat-laden fried bread, yum yum.

Ps. Probably the reason I had a cardiac stent inserted last year.

Paul Houghton FRCS
Sigford, Devon

SIR — I shall know that the barbarians are at the gate when marmalade with toast gives way to jam.

Maxwell Blake
London SW3

The bottom line

SIR — My daughter, as a teenager, overused the quilted lavatory paper — so I labelled every three or four sheets with the days of the week.

Giles Smith
Bury St Edmunds, Suffolk

SIR — In the 1940s it was always a pleasure to visit my aunt's outside lavatory where hung cut pages of my cousins' *Beano*. It was a challenge to reassemble a complete comic strip.

Wyllan M. Horsfall
Sheffield, South Yorkshire

A new cold war

SIR — Having seen the astronomical new rates from our energy supplier, I wonder whether it might be cheaper to cut out the middleman and burn banknotes to heat the house.

Richard Cheeseman
Yateley, Hampshire

SIR – I would like to write a long letter about rising energy costs but I am busy lifting floorboards to make a fire.

Charlotte Joseph
Lawford, Essex

SIR – I know now what "net zero" means. It refers to the temperature in my house.

Stephen Simpson
Bath, Somerset

SIR – I never cease to be surprised by the Chancellor's inventiveness.

My understanding of the latest energy rebate scheme is that I am to be compelled to lend myself the sum of £200.

Then I am to be compelled to repay myself at the rate of £40 per year for five years.

I am just trying to work out what rate of interest I should charge myself.

Jeff Hornsey
Ringstead, Northamptonshire

SIR – Turn off the heating in Parliament and No 10.

That should concentrate minds on the plight of ordinary folk.

Chris Thompson
Huddersfield, West Yorkshire

SIR – Air source heat pumps have a lot in common with the heater in my 1954 Morris Minor. It only seems to work well in the summer.

Geoff Pursglove
Swadlincote, South Derbyshire

SIR – Over a long weekend with intermittent electricity, we enjoyed our dark evenings watching the guttering candles. The last straw was that the only light in the house was on the smart meter.

Kay East
Tonbridge, Kent

SIR – We've consigned our smart meter monitor to a cupboard, believing there's not much to be gained from torturing ourselves daily. I feel better already.

Jill Pick
Driffield, East Yorkshire

Crying all the way to the bank

SIR – I've just had an envelope containing two pieces of paper from my local bank. The first said: "We're Here to Help".

The second said: "We're Closing Your Branch". Thanks!

David Booth
Latheron, Caithness

SIR – I had a china money box in the shape of a
crown at the time of the Queen's coronation in 1953.
Much of my pocket money went into it, until it was
full. There was no way of getting the coins out without
breaking the money box, which I duly did. I then used
all the money I had saved to buy another money box.
This was my first lesson in basic economics.

Nigel Johnson-Hill
Petersfield, Hampshire

SIR – The Bank of England has redrawn its logo
to reflect its "current mission and values". Sadly,
its main mission to contain inflation has been
less than satisfactory. However, this is presumably
demonstrated by the removal of the pile of coins at
Britannia's feet.

Cameron Morice
Reading, Berkshire

SIR – I have come up with a suitable alternative
investment to cryptocurrencies: tulips. Why has no
one thought of that before?

Gordon Brown
Grassington, North Yorkshire

SIR – It seems that the only way to make a small
fortune in Bitcoin is to start with a big fortune in
Bitcoin.

Robert Ward
Loughborough, Leicestershire

SIR – I have just received my annual notification of my state pension benefits. There is a note advising me that from my 80th birthday I shall receive an additional 25p a week.

I have ordered a new Ferrari.

Robin Beynon
London SW14

SIR – About a year ago I rescued a feral cat on our farm. I have tamed her and named her Tuppence. Due to the increase in inflation, my husband has renamed her Threepence.

Linda Booth
Doncaster, South Yorkshire

SIR – I can't believe that the Government's advice to survive inflation is to get a better job.

I am fortunate to be in good health but I don't think anyone would want to employ an 86-year-old pensioner. Any offers?

Rosemary Reed
Woodhall Spa, Lincolnshire

SIR – Wouldn't news headlines be more useful in telling us who isn't going on strike at the moment?

J. S. F. Cash
Swinford, Leiceistershire

SIR – Faced with a diminishing income and rapidly increasing prices, my wife and I have reluctantly decided to go on strike.

I trust we will shortly receive a 30 per cent pay rise.

Joe Greaves
Fleckney, Leicestershire

SIR – We should all go on strike and eventually die of starvation, lack of medication or pure boredom. Then there would be a welcome quietness and any personal injustice felt would be totally irrelevant.

Peter Dimery
Newport, Monmouthshire

SIR – We shall know that the cost of living crisis is really hitting home when the streets are no longer full of people carrying takeaway coffees.

Patricia Reid
Chipping Campden, Gloucestershire

Not-so-smart technology

SIR – I was reading emails on my new mobile phone, which is packed with a daunting array of features I know nothing of and will never use, when a dog jumped up beside me on the sofa, demanding attention.

I said to the dog, "You are being rather a pest", and the phone said, "I am sorry about that. I will do better next time."

Tim Nicholson
Cranbrook, Kent

SIR – Seeing the baked marmalade roll extolled on the *Telegraph* Letters Page prompted me to send an email about it to a friend who is always on the lookout for ideas to extend her cook's repertoire.

She replied immediately thanking me for suggesting marmalade roll but querying why it had to be cooked in the nude. That was the first time I noticed that *b* and *n* are next to one another on a QWERTY keyboard.

Bruce Denness
Niton, Isle of Wight

SIR – In the early days of computer spellcheck I completed a job application form only to have the zealous desktop helpfully change my name to Weedy Fabrication.

Two of my friends still call me this.

Wendy Farrington
Kendal, Cumbria

SIR – I once sent a business email to a senior manager that started "Dear Anal". Fortunately Alan took it in good humour and we remained on good terms.

Bill Crichton
Crewe, Cheshire

SIR – Not only does computers' spelling often leave a lot to be desired, there proof readings knot marvel louse.

Anne Jappie
Cheltenham, Gloucestershire

Unexpected items in the bagging area

SIR – In order to test, record and measure my physical and mental dexterity, I have a simple but infuriating yardstick.

How many items can you swipe at the Waitrose checkout before the high-pitched instruction of "Please scan an item or press finish and pay" is issued?

My record is five.

Howard Jones
Cheltenham, Gloucestershire

SIR – One wonders the extent to which *The Great British Sewing Bee* has influenced our online retailers. The confirmation email from M&S for a single dress placed by my wife contained this paragraph:

"Please note, your order may be dispatched from multiple locations and therefore could arrive in separate deliveries."

A mannequin and sewing machine have been placed on standby should our worst nightmares materialise.

John Illidge
Northwich, Cheshire

Stylish, after a fashion

SIR – *The Daily Telegraph* is to be congratulated for publishing the photograph of the latest offering from Paris Fashion Week. Now, more than ever, we need a belly laugh.

> **Brian Inns**
> Melksham, Wiltshire

SIR – I am amazed at the miserable expressions of models at the various fashion shows. Some of the outfits they wear are so ridiculous that they should be laughing their heads off.

> **Rona Taylor**
> Bristol

SIR – Melania Trump has expressed concern that *Vogue* may be biased against her as it hasn't asked her to be on the front page. Maybe *Vogue* does have some biases as the magazine has never asked me to appear on the cover either. This is possibly related to my being a 63-year-old, fat, bald man with the general appearance of a biker.

I'm not holding a grudge and am still ready to make my own unique contribution to the fashion world.

> **Dennis Fitzgerald**
> Melbourne, Australia

SIR – I was surprised to read the headline to Tamara Abraham's article: "Yes, you can buy a forever bag for under £350". I recently purchased a cotton "bag for life" from Morrisons for only £2.50, which clearly meets the criteria set out – "…it needs to be well constructed, using quality materials in a relatively timeless shape."

Tobias Woolfitt
Shefford, Bedfordshire

SIR – Why are clothes presented for sale with the shortest garments at the top of the pile and the longest at the bottom? I ask this on behalf of all those who are vertically challenged.

Nicholas Fowle
Neatishead, Norfolk

SIR – Your newspaper speaks of the possibility of a return to the inflationary and strike-ridden times last seen in the 1970s. While such an outcome should be avoided if at all possible, one step would command almost universal support: legislation to prevent any return of 1970s fashion. Mullets, sideburns, flares, brown clothes and platforms have no place in a modern society.

Tim Reid
Mayfield, East Sussex

SIR – Jane Shilling's piece on the decline of sartorial standards during lockdown reminded me of my surprise during a visit to the ITN studios, when I observed the newsreader Trevor Phillips reading his news bulletin immaculately dressed on top – and sporting a pair of denim jeans from the waist down.

Diana Jones
Via email

SIR – I remember saying to my West Yorkshire grandmother, "Look at that gentleman over there in the brown suit."

"Gentlemen do not wear brown suits", was her reply.

Nicholas Franks
Dorchester, Dorset

SIR – Is the ubiquitous blue suit a natural segue from red trousers? And when will the fad for the ageing beard, particularly those with pepper and salt, cease? Oh to see a smartly dressed, clean-shaven man!

Diana Spencer
Herne Bay, Kent

SIR – Few things enhance the looks of a good man (or bad) so much as a good suit. A glimpse of such apparel improves my day no end and gives a sprightly lift to my evening cocktail.

Suzette Hill
Ledbury, Herefordshire

SIR — My father, who always wore a vest, shirt, tie and daily polished shoes until he was 93, said to me when I was a teenager that you can tell a man's character by the state of his shoes. Needless to say I stopped polishing mine.

Keith Allum
Christchurch, Dorset

SIR — Do all socks shrink by the same amount?

Bill Welland
Somerton, Somerset

Keeping up appearances

SIR — I was intrigued to read that an underwired bra could make me look taller and slimmer.
　　Perhaps I should investigate further.

Paul Holland
Bognor Regis, West Sussex

SIR — My mother instilled in us from an early age that underwear, especially knickers, had to be ironed in case one should be run over.
　　I still prepare for this eventuality.

Dr Lynda Taylor
Bury, Lancashire

SIR – My grandmother taught me that the mark of a lady was that if the elastic in her knickers should fail and they fell down, she would step out of them, with her head held high, and carry on.

Trish Galli
Shaldon, Devon

SIR – My 97-year-old aunt was amused to see the photograph of the naked festival goers at Glastonbury.

She told me that her late husband walked naked quite often through their Hampshire village and allegedly once managed to get served in their local pub. Apparently he wore only a large fedora which he delighted in raising every time he met other parishioners.

Stephen Hewitt
Pulham Market, Norfolk

SIR – My late mother had two sets of dentures. One set was better for chewing food, while the second set provided superior aesthetic qualities.

For inexplicable reasons, prior to using the telephone, she would always make sure she was wearing her "smiling teeth".

Graham Hoyle
Shipley, West Yorkshire

Age is just a number

SIR – Today is a beautiful day. Not only is the sun shining, but the obituaries are all for people over the age of 90; two were over 99.

I am pushing 80 and for me this is good news.

Maureen West
Bovingdon, Hertfordshire

SIR – Recently I was on the phone to an insurance company on behalf of my mother-in-law, aged 102. I was asked her date of birth which I gave as 2 July 1919. A few seconds later I was asked to give details of her occupation. "She's a freefall parachute instructor," I explained. Silence.

Eldon Sandys
Pyrford, Surrey

SIR – Very shortly before his death my father was involved in a minor road accident.

He died from totally unrelated causes before he could contact his insurance company.

As his executor, I checked with his insurance company as to what action was needed to make a claim on his insurance for damage to the car.

After a lengthy telephone interrogation, I was told that there would be no problems but that I would need to bring my father to the telephone to confirm what I had told them.

I resisted the temptation to raise the subject of travelling expenses.

John Reynolds
Nottingham

SIR – As the executor for my late father's will, I received a formal letter which began:
  "Dear Mr Henderson D'Ceased".

Colin Henderson
Cranleigh, Surrey

SIR – I am an active older lady and I often mutter "Daft old biddy" to myself, but I swear I will punch the lights out of the next person who says "Ah, bless!" to me.

Chris Gordon
Boston, Lincolnshire

SIR – Over the various lockdowns my husband has morphed into Victor Meldrew. When confronted he simply says, "I don't believe it!" Case proven I'm afraid.

Jackie Mullens
Chertsey, Surrey

SIR — I am pleased to read that science has caught up with my own theory that memory loss in older age may stem from the brain being too cluttered with knowledge. I formed this theory some time ago as the only way to explain why, occasionally, I found myself searching the fridge for my tennis shoes.

Steve Goodman
Leicester

SIR — My wife has just noticed when putting on socks that her feet have become more distant with age.

A. Eastwood
Bromley, Kent

SIR — Instructions on a newly purchased Zimmer frame: "Do not clean using lighter fuel". Is someone paid to think outside the box?

Sue Hamilton-Miller
Twickenham, Middlesex

Papa was a rolling stone

SIR – Allister Heath says that British people are not having enough children. However, you cannot say that Mick Jagger has not done his best.

Paul Jones
Radcliffe-on-Trent, Nottinghamshire

SIR – Could *The Daily Telegraph* please run more articles by Shane Watson on "How to have more sex"? Not for the content, but for the online comments. My wife hasn't laughed as much for ages!

Toby Stobart
Malaga, Spain

SIR – When I was at school in the 1950s our sex education was demonstrated using the procreation process of the rabbit, with diagrams. At the end of the very embarrassing lesson, our teacher just said, "And it is the same for humans."

The effect on 30 12-year-old girls was mixed, and some of us are still hopping around in fields looking for real love.

Isobel Barker
Torpoint, Cornwall

SIR – The young biology master who caught us *in flagrante delicto* nobly remained silent on the subject, but his comment in my school report said, "He appears to have no interest in the subject in class, but seemingly has a flair for practical work."

John Bath
Clevedon, North Somerset

SIR – As a young newly married couple living in Zimbabwe in the early 1970s, my husband and I witnessed a pair of praying mantis having rumpy pumpy, after which the female mantis promptly turned around and bit off his head.

My husband has treated me with the greatest respect ever since.

Jean Routledge
Roker, Sunderland

The things we do for love

SIR – Every day my wife and I avidly read your recipe newsletter and often try some of the recipes. So when today's newsletter arrived at 2.15pm (3.15pm Dutch time) I was delighted to read your recommendations for tonight's special Valentine's Day meal.

Now I just have enough time to go out and find the necessary oysters and lobster tail before coming home and baking the molten salted caramel chocolate tart

– which, I see, has to be chilled for two hours before eating. Looks like a busy afternoon.

Alun Harvey
Groningen, The Netherlands

SIR – I have received an email from Facebook recommending me to join a group called "Facebook Dating Online for Singles." I am a 99-year-old widower living in a care home. Something wrong with their algorithm?

Keith Herdman
London SE3

Names to conjure with

SIR – A new worry:

"People called Michael and Emma are the most likely to end up in prison" (report, 5 May).

Michael Nicholson
Petworth, West Sussex

SIR – Our eldest grandson had a narrow escape. He was to be named after two of his great-grandfathers. In the middle of the night before he was born my wife suddenly sat up in bed: "They can't name him that!!"

He was to be called Richard Edward. He is now called James.

Patrick Brady
Peak District, Derbyshire

SIR – My cousin's surname is Wright. His wife is fondly known as Always.

Alan Tomlinson
Cheadle, Cheshire

We don't need no education

SIR – As my daughter approaches the end of her GCSE exams I would like to congratulate the examination boards for preparing our children perfectly for modern working life. At my workplace I am regularly locked in a room for 90 minutes with no access to the Internet and told to hand-write a report. The warning issued to pupils before each exam that blotting paper is not allowed in the exam room is particularly welcome and relevant in the 21st century.

Victor Arotsky
London NW4

SIR – The headmaster's comment on my school report (c.1954) was as follows:
  "If this boy's mind is as original as his spelling, he should go far".

James Ayres FSA
Bath, Somerset

SIR – My son's school report once credited him with "rapidly evaporating good intentions".

Captain Graham Sullivan RN (retd)
Eye, Suffolk

SIR – The comment I best recall from my school reports of the early 1960s was: "Christopher has had a restful term".

Chris King
Woking, Surrey

SIR – I found maths hard in the 1960s and took my maths O level five times with five failures.

My solution to this was to marry an accountant.

Beverley White
Northwood, Middlesex

SIR – I wholly disagree with the notion that attending a boarding school is damaging.

Boarding school teaches our young people two vital rules of life. First, how to get dressed quickly in the morning and, secondly, never to get caught.

Roger Collings
Presteign, Radnorshire

SIR – I see that universities are now to issue trigger warnings for some classic novels. Good luck to anyone who takes on compiling trigger warnings for the Bible; they will have a big job on their hands.

Jenny Furness
Doncaster, South Yorkshire

SIR — It has long been obvious that *Romeo and Juliet* should not be taught in schools. Teenagers carrying knives for street violence, breaking and entering for underage sex, tripping on illegal substances leading to self-harm — it's a total disgrace!

R. Allan Reese
Dorchester

SIR — I was amused to read that students at Durham have called for an end to "sinister" formal dinners.

My memories of attending in the 1990s are of table-banging with the cutlery, the compulsory eating of desserts without a spoon, and a life lesson for one of my friends — never to wear a white tuxedo in a food fight involving blackcurrant blancmange.

James Trask
Berkhamsted, Hertfordshire

SIR — I was at university in the early 1960s, and we had formal dinners in the hall of residence on Sundays. Many of us found the flowing black gowns a useful cover-up for our nightwear, or — in summer — our shorts and T-shirts (or less).

Carolyn Andrews
Bournemouth, Dorset

SIR — I would be very sad for Barts medical school to lose its unique identity. Will we never again be able to sing "The Barts Song" much beloved of the rugby teams of the other medical schools?

It is a very simple song sung to the tune of "The Dambusters March". The words are as follows:

> We all hate Barts,
> And Barts and Barts,
> And Barts and Barts,
> And Barts and Barts,
> And Barts and Barts,
> We all f-----g hate Barts,
> We all hate Barts,
> And Barts...

This should be sung ad nauseam or until someone from Barts responds.

David Bennett FRCGP
Holt, Norfolk

Give them an inch

SIR – As an "older" engineer, I was taught mechanics using imperial units and I would certainly not want to have to use them again. However, if Boris Johnson succeeds in his latest ridiculous attempt to restore an ounce of his waning popularity, perhaps I will make a point of using one unit of mass – the slug.

Norman Burrow
Preston, Lancashire

SIR – It's good news for the inchworm.

"Twenty-five point four millimetre worm" is a bit of a mouthful.

Rowley Kempson
Bovey Tracey, Devon

SIR – Boris Johnson's idea to return to imperial measures might backfire when people realise that petrol costs an eye-watering £7.50 per gallon.

Wendy Bentall
Chobham, Surrey

Have a little faith

SIR – Given the Archbishop of Canterbury's recent forays into politics, may I ask when he next proposes to go into retreat?

It can't come a day too soon.

Mike Tugby
Warminster, Wiltshire

SIR – We receive a weekly bulletin from our local church giving the details of the week's services. This week it included instructions for donations to our forthcoming fête:

"Gods to donate – please contact the stallholder or leave them in the boxes under the Beaufort tower as near to fête day as possible."

Celia Harris
Winchester, Hampshire

SIR – I once dropped a joke into a conversation with my then parish priest, saying that I had heard the Oxford English Dictionary was removing the word "gullible" from its listings. He exclaimed, "No!" followed by, "----ing hell!" Men first, priests second.

Sandra Hancock
Exeter, Devon

I wonder where the birdies is?

SIR – Over the years many people have written to say that they have heard the first cuckoo of the year. Today (24 March), I heard the first ice-cream van melody.

James Brosnan
Rochester, Kent

SIR – I have seen my first swallow of summer – flying inside a Tesco store in Norwich on Monday 2 May.

Susan Hewitt
Pulham Market, Norfolk

SIR – I have just witnessed two ring-necked parakeets having a loud argument with a grey squirrel. I couldn't help wondering which was accusing the other of being the unwanted foreigner.

Brian Gedalla
London N3

SIR – A headline in your news bulletin reads:
"Birdsong may be good for your mental health".
I have a blackbird that sings outside my bedroom
window at 4.40am, which is definitely not good
for my health, mental or otherwise. It may turn out
to be bad for the blackbird's health as well.

Peter Wickison
Driffield, East Yorkshire

There may be trouble ahead

SIR – I would like to express my thanks to BBC
Breakfast for explaining that a flood warning means
that there may be flooding. I had been pondering
that for several days.

Phil Corrigan
St Albans, Hertfordshire

SIR – My wife has just informed me that Storm
Eunice wishes to self-identify as a hurricane.

Simon Conway
Ringstead, Northamptonshire

SIR – Wind garden sale: fence panels, trampolines,
patio chairs.
  New stuff arriving all the time.

Brendon Chappell
Bexhill-on-Sea, East Sussex

SIR – It seems that, after Storm Eunice, the Millennium Dome has gone the same way as all the other New Labour initiatives.

Gregory Shenkman
London SW7

SIR – Yet again the travelling public has been inconvenienced by cancellations on the railways due to leaves on the line. This time, they were attached to trees.

Malcolm Goldie
Hildenborough, Kent

SIR – My insurance company has refused my claim for storm damage repairs, claiming it was an act of God and therefore excluded from the cover. As it is an act of God, may I make a claim via the Archbishop of Canterbury?

Alan Belk
Leatherhead, Surrey

Here comes the sun

SIR – Hammersmith Bridge has been covered in tin foil to keep it cool this summer. I assume a tea cosy is being knitted in readiness for the severe cold in the winter.

Edwina Rickards Collinson
Capernwray, Lancashire

SIR – With extreme heat forecast for the next few days, I am planning a weekend away in the frozen food aisle of my local supermarket.

Dave Bassett
Liverpool

SIR – I wore a necktie every school day and work day for 50 years. The heatwave has confirmed my opinion on its absurdity and uselessness.

Lee Goodall
Churchdown, Gloucestershire

SIR – I have adapted to the heat.

I have ordered four mini-kegs of Adnams' excellent Ghost Ship bitter.

John Cooper
Southwold, Suffolk

SIR – It was good to read the memories of the 1976 drought. I recall the downpours shortly after Denis Howell's appointment as Minister for Drought. Most of all I remember the numerous subsequent demands to make Howell Chancellor of the Exchequer. Our financial woes of the time, it was suggested, would immediately be solved by a deluge of cash.

Paul Barnett
Corsham, Wiltshire

SIR – Back in the summer heatwave of 1976, the thought of sharing five inches of bath water with my wife would most definitely have got me in a lather.

Today, it would be a very different story. The combination of arthritic knees, dodgy hips and jointly elevated BMIs would make the task difficult to say the least.

Pre-greasing the bath like a pie dish may be the only way to prevent a call to emergency services – but that would defeat the object.

Gary Freestone
Leicester

SIR – Heatwave? It's summer. It's supposed to be hot.

Sandra Hancock
Exeter, Devon

SIR – I don't think that we need to worry too much about the present drought, as it will surely end on 17 August.

How can I be so certain? It is the first day of the Lord's Test Match, and I have tickets.

Gavin Choyce
London W2

Born to be wild

SIR – I was wondering whether the success of a rewilding garden at Chelsea this year had anything to do with the fact that the president of the Royal Horticultural Society is a Mr Weed.

Penny Stewart
Sherborne, Dorset

SIR – Inspired by the rewilding garden that won the top prize, I'd like to have a go at incorporating some of these ideas into my own modest plot. Can anyone tell me if beavers make good pets and whether they like vegetables or not?

Frances Kirby-Johnson
Marlborough, Wiltshire

SIR – If the judges from the Chelsea Flower Show would like to visit my hometown, I can show them examples where nature has "rewilded" areas, generally in front of empty or derelict houses.

Granville Pugh
Rugeley, Staffordshire

Growing pains

SIR – A local council has banned the planting of daffodils for fear that children may poison themselves by eating them.

During many years of nursing the worst encounter I ever had with a dangerous daffodil was when a worried mother accompanied by her young son arrived at my medicines information centre with a daffodil stalk and head stuck firmly up his nose.

Helen Price
Blackpool

SIR – I know a dear, kind gentleman friend who was arrested in the 1970s at Schiphol Airport for eating several daffodils.

Admittedly, he had also drunk 20 vodkas on the 40-minute flight from England and he was incapable of standing.

My point is that eating daffodils, in themselves, is not necessarily harmful.

Chris Bird
Frome, Somerset

SIR – Having been relieved of the tyranny of lawn-mowing through No Mow May, I now need to convince my wife that, for ecological reasons, this has been extended into Jungle June.

Chris Read
Guildford, Surrey

SIR – We have all been observing No Mow May. It is a pity that my dog has not provided me with No Poo May to go along with it. It has been increasingly difficult to clear up the mess and I shall be glad when we get to June.

David Sidebotham
Hayling Island, Hampshire

SIR – I have been left wondering why it is that when I prune the plants, shrubs and bushes in my garden I seem to end up with more than I started with.

Robert Ashworth
Alderley Edge, Cheshire

SIR – I mentioned to my husband that recent letters regarding the use of the scythe brought back fond memories of *Poldark*, and especially Aidan Turner.

In (I suppose) his attempt to impress me, my husband came out of our garden shed brandishing a long-lost scythe. He proceeded to cut the front grass verge, stripped to the waist, but being a septuagenarian, the visual impact was not quite the same as in *Poldark*. It also had unforeseen consequences for the road traffic.

> **Carol Belk**
> Leatherhead, Surrey

SIR – Why is it that wherever you stand in relation to a bonfire, the smoke knows where you are?

> **Carey Waite**
> Melksham, Wiltshire

SIR – I used to enjoy the autumn, until the invention of leaf blowers.

> **John Noble**
> Kingston upon Thames, Surrey

Pets corner

SIR – Fat cats have always been around and some have brought us felines into disrepute. At the age of 12 I remain handsome, lithe and athletic, regularly patrolling my territory and often running at speed to see off marauding birds and squirrels and to catch mice. I can leap ten feet onto the summerhouse roof.

Regular meals and such exercise keeps us healthy cats fit, even though some are a little chubby.

George the cat

C/o John Pritchard
Ingatestone, Essex

SIR – In rural Nigeria, our neighbours were shocked that we kept such an unclean creature as a cat in our home. I argued that cats spent a lot of time cleaning themselves. They shot down my argument by asking what with.

Rev Dr John S. Ross
Drumnadrochit, Inverness-shire

SIR – My husband likes to pop down to our local pub most days to have a glass of wine. Our Irish wolfhound likes to go as well and sits in the car in the square of our local village with the window open to watch the world go by while the Lord and Master is refreshing himself.

This week my husband had Covid, so obviously did not go. Day one and day two went by, and the wolfhound sat by the car to no avail.

Yesterday, day three, the dog could not stand it any longer – he jumped in and out of the back of the car several times, woofing very pointedly. My husband relented and drove to the square, parked the car outside the pub for 10 minutes and sat browsing his smartphone. Result, one happy contented dog.

Mrs M. Williams
St Keverne, Cornwall

SIR – Rarely do I fail in my daily quest to find a
news story in *The Daily Telegraph* that would be worthy
of inclusion as a spoof item on 1 April.

Today's is the report of vets telling owners to
provide sunglasses for their dogs.

Richard Frost
Berkhamsted, Hertfordshire

SIR – If the Welsh Government refuses to change
the law that bans dog collars which deliver an electric
shock when dogs chase sheep, maybe the owners
should be compelled to wear them instead.

Anne Omer
Banbury, Oxfordshire

SIR – There seems to be a proliferation of dogs
wearing jackets, woollies and in some cases socks/leg
warmers. Is it a fashion statement? If so, perhaps the
dog walk will take over from the catwalk.

Geoffrey Moody
Harrietsham, Kent

SIR – Christmas is always a dangerous time for our
canine friends with the proliferation of chocolate
around the house.

This year a friend messaged me disclosing that
Bugsy the beagle had eaten a chocolate Santa Claus.
She was, however, quick to allay my fears.

"That's nothing! At Easter he had two chocolate oranges and a light bulb."

Janet Newis
Sidcup, Kent

It is the season

SIR — My grown-up children play a Whamageddon competition each December based on Wham!'s "Last Christmas".

The winner is the last one to hear it.

Rosemary Cowie
Brighton, East Sussex

SIR — I have yet to hear the Christmas record "Frosty the Snowman". Another effect of global warming?

Raymond Short
Baughurst, Hampshire

SIR — We are now into what seems to be the umpteenth season of Ronan Collins on RTE Radio I playing a different version of "O Holy Night" on all the days leading up to Christmas.

Should we be thankful he didn't choose "Rudolph the Red-Nosed Reindeer" instead?

Liam Power
Dundalk, Co Louth, Ireland

SIR – I am reassured to learn that even the gifted actor Sir Antony Sher was actually rejected by Rada. In his first Nativity play, my grandson (aged three) has been cast as "Door".

C. D. Henderson
Cranleigh, Surrey

SIR – I have just read your articles about what I can expect to see on the television on Christmas Day. All I can say is, what a good excuse to get stuck into my drinks cabinet. It's either that or talk to my wife. Where's the corkscrew?

Mike Tugby
Warminster, Wiltshire

Present difficulty

SIR – When browsing with my three daughters in a toy shop this weekend, the youngest marvelled at a beautiful life-sized Bambi with a price tag of £1,600. I quickly pointed out to her that this was much too expensive for a Christmas present. She smiled and said, "Don't worry Daddy; if Santa gets it for me you won't have to pay anything."

Nick Smith
London SW6

SIR – In the 1960s, hoping for a drum kit, I received an empty shoe box for Christmas. I was told it was an Action Man deserter by my parents.

Ian Rennardson
Tunbridge Wells, Kent

SIR – Soon after my divorce around Christmas 1983, I got a "His" monogrammed bath towel as a present. I wonder if my ex-wife got the "Hers" one.

James Logan
Portstewart, Co Londonderry

SIR – I was given a rain gauge for Christmas which came with the advice: "For outdoor use only".

Linda Sykes
Waltham St Lawrence, Berkshire

SIR – My daughter was given a fondue set for Christmas. The side-effects read: "ask your mother-in-law or the postman".

Ann Roberts
Market Harborough, Leicestershire

A YEAR IN
POLITICS

The honour is all theirs

SIR – Charles Moore recalls that Harold Macmillan twice refused the Garter. The appointment of Tony Blair to the Order leads me to support Lord Melbourne's view: "What I like about the Order of the Garter is that there is no damned merit about it."

Merrick Baker-Bates
Creaton, Northamptonshire

SIR – Tony Blair will now become even more insufferable.
How is that possible?

Robin Lane
Devizes, Wiltshire

SIR – Of course Tony Blair should be made a Knight of the Garter. Otherwise, in a hundred years' time there could be a shortage of historical figures for future generations to cancel.

Will Doran
High Wycombe, Buckinghamshire

SIR – While serving nearly 48 years for the MoD,
I'm sure I must have made more cock-ups than
Sir Gavin Williamson. Can I have a knighthood too,
please?

> **Rob Dorrell**
> Bath, Somerset

SIR – My attempts at gardening and DIY are
notoriously unsuccessful. Do I have to apply for my
well-earned knighthood, or do I just wait for someone
to give it to me?

> **Robin Nonhebel**
> Swanage, Dorset

SIR – Having survived to the age of 75 I am relieved
that I have never suffered the ignominy of being
offered a knighthood.

> **Roy Vickers**
> Berkhamsted, Hertfordshire

Today in Westminster

SIR – I am currently enjoying the unpublished letters to *The Daily Telegraph* in *Has the World Gone Completely Mad…?*, printed in 2015.

One section refers to MPs' greed, scandals, lack of integrity, referrals to the Parliamentary Standards Committee and generally immoral conduct. In seven years MPs really have radically improved their behaviour, haven't they?

Rob Baldock
Boston, Lincolnshire

SIR – Some of our MPs deserve to lose the title Right Honourable. It should be replaced with Right So and So.

Bernard Powell
Southport, Lancashire

SIR – I've coined a new collective noun: an arrogance of politicians.

Elizabeth Griffin
Shrewsbury, Shropshire

SIR – I remember as a boy in the 1960s being taken to Regent's Park Zoo where my favourite spectacle was always the chimpanzees' tea party. Never did I imagine that one day they would be running the government of the country I love and have fought for, as well as – it has to be said – occupying all of the Opposition benches.

Major Nigel Price (retd)
Wilmslow, Cheshire

SIR – I read that there is to be an exhibition in London which encourages sleepiness. There has already been such a phenomenon in existence for many years. It is called the House of Lords.

Rupert Wilson
Shepley, West Yorkshire

State of fear

SIR – I shall miss the regular apocalyptic blood-curdling predictions from the Scientific Advisory Group for Emergencies, and instead content myself with old Hammer films and the Horror Channel.

Tony Manning
Barton on Sea, Hampshire

SIR – I cannot understand why the epidemiologist Neil Ferguson should be allowed to continue his predictions of doom, given his track record over several years. Perhaps he could be allowed out annually at Halloween, given that he is so good at scaring the living daylights out of people.

> **Sue Milne**
> Crick, Northamptonshire

SIR – Watching the Government's response to the coronavirus pandemic is akin to watching a very long episode of *Dad's Army*. Unfortunately, Private Frazer has just taken centre stage again.

> **Oliver Tyson**
> Ashby-de-la-Zouch, Leicestershire

SIR – In our risk-averse, hyper-cautious society, the mantra "Keep calm and carry on" should perhaps now be changed to "Become hysterical and stop everything".

> **Keith Whittaker**
> Newcastle-under-Lyme, Staffordshire

SIR – I await with bated breath the publication of Sage's official snogging traffic light system. It can only be a matter of time.

> **Mark Calvin FCII**
> Crickhowell, Powys

SIR – I would like to express my gratitude to
Matt Hancock and Allegra Stratton for the part they
have played in releasing large swathes of the public
from the fear-induced hypnotic trance holding them
sway since March 2020.

Victoria Edge
Farningham, Kent

SIR – We have been told not to panic about the
Omicron mutation. Apparently panic is now reserved
for the Government. I am a taxpayer, I am fully
vaccinated, and if I want to panic, it is my right.
After all that we have been through we deserve a good
panic, if only to relieve the tedium of stiffening
our upper lips at what appear to be ever-shortening
intervals. PANIC IS NOT A GOVERNMENT
MONOPOLY.

C. Williams
Coedpoeth, Wrexham

SIR – It is surely of considerable concern that even
President Joe Biden's utterances on the Omicron
variant are far more sensible than those of our
Prime Minister and his Health Secretary. It certainly
worries me.

Ian Goddard
Wickham, Hampshire

SIR – I would like to suggest a clue for your crossword: Government makes moronic move for variant. (Anag.)

Barrie Bain
Wadhurst, East Sussex

SIR – I wonder if the World Health Organisation has given any consideration as to how future variants of the coronavirus will be named once they have reached the end of the Greek alphabet.

Garry P. High
Guildford, Surrey

SIR – If we are to see a return to regular Covid briefings from Downing Street, perhaps the Prime Minister could take Peppa Pig and Suzy Sheep along with him instead of his scientific advisers and Cabinet colleagues.

I know who I am more likely to believe.

Martyn Pitt
Gloucester

SIR – I used to take flowers or a box of chocolates to a dinner party. In future I will take a coveted box of lateral flow tests.

Sandra Summerfield
Newcastle upon Tyne

SIR – I see that Sir Keir Starmer is self-isolating for the sixth time – will anybody notice?

Ian Franklin
Totnes, Devon

The road to recovery

SIR – Now that most of the population has had its Covid jabs, it is about time the NHS itself had a shot in the arm to restore our general health services. Perhaps a new motto would be a good start. I suggest: "Patients are a virtue".

Timothy Jordan
Bristol

SIR – The National Audit Office reports that the NHS now has 5.9 million people on its waiting lists.

I worked in the Hotel and Catering industry, which is roughly the size of the whole NHS, for over 25 years, but we never had 5.9 million customers waiting for their breakfasts.

Perhaps hoteliers should be asked to run the NHS.

Tony Tighe
Devizes, Wiltshire

SIR – NHS – Notional Health Service.

John Micklewright
Weston, Cheshire

SIR – Labour's Emily Thornberry has announced that she would not date anyone who has not been jabbed. I have been triple-jabbed. Am I safe?

Jo Bird
Slapton, Devon

SIR – I've solved it: let's make vaccine passports mandatory BUT have the DVLA issue them.

That should prevent the spread of Covid at the mere cost of making us all prisoners in our homes.

Mark Hodson
Bristol

Tax and spend, spend, spend

SIR – Prior to the 1997 general election, John Prescott in positioning New Labour is said to have made the quip: "We're all middle class now."

Given the Spring Statement and the Conservatives' addiction to tax and spend policies, I am waiting for Boris Johnson to quip: "We're all socialists now."

Rupert Mindelsohn
Marlborough, Wiltshire

SIR – The Chancellor seems to think that he can tax us back to prosperity. He also seems to think that voters will thank him for it.

He is wrong on both counts.

Matthew Brown
Shaftesbury, Dorset

SIR — There was much mention of hard-working people in the Chancellor's statement. Now that the Tories have adopted this description of the working class — which used to be the exclusive preserve of the Labour Party — I wonder which party will stand up for the rights of idle gits like me. We are the forgotten many.

Alan Hollowood
Blandford Forum, Dorset

SIR — Your front-page headline describes a windfall tax on energy companies as "wildly popular".

We should not forget that in March 2020 lockdown was wildly popular. We have had plenty of time to regret that action since.

John Murray
Guildford, Surrey

SIR — Free beer for all would be "wildly popular". It doesn't make it the right thing to do.

David A. E. Beedell
Rochester, Kent

SIR — Every 40 years Britain needs a dose of Thatcherism: like some medicines, it might not taste nice but it's good for you.

Guy Williamson
Colchester, Essex

SIR – My wife has offered to kick me out if it would help me become non-domiciled for tax purposes.

Alexander Williams
Kingston upon Thames, Surrey

SIR – There is a simple way to satisfy critics claiming that Rishi Sunak is "too rich to be Chancellor".
Just appoint some lifelong failures who have never made any money, created any wealth or been in any way "successful".

The ranks of backbenchers of all parties could provide a surfeit of candidates.

Ken Torkington
Abergavenny, Monmouthshire

Feeling blue

SIR – Can anyone tell me where the Conservative Party has gone?

I have financially supported it, campaigned for it, defended it, represented it and held public office on its behalf.

But I can't find it anywhere. Perhaps it will resurface, like Plymouth's woolly mammoths, in another thirty thousand years.

Chris McLaughlin
London SW19

SIR – I woke up in the middle of last night following a nightmare about the prospect of having a high-tax, high-spending socialist government in power after the next election.

I soon realised that we already have one, so went back to sleep again.

Graham Jones
Tytherington, Cheshire

SIR – I'm a Conservative. Get me out of here!

David Plummer
Great Alne, Warwickshire

SIR – Is the current infighting in the Conservative Party the reason why ministers are invariably pictured wearing hard hats these days?

Richard Cooke
Reepham, Norfolk

SIR – The Conservative Party has a new slogan. "Vote for us and you can have government AND opposition". The only thing it needs now is an effective leader.

Ian Forster
Wakefield, West Yorkshire

SIR – Meta Platforms continues to be referred to as: Meta, formerly known as Facebook.

Given the Tory Government has departed from all things conservative, perhaps it too is due a rebrand.

The _ _ _ Government, formerly known as the Conservative Party.

I will leave it to your dear readers to fill in the blanks.

James Bisset
London SW4

SIR – How clever of the Monster Raving Loony Party to have occupied 10 Downing Street.

Duncan Christie-Miller
Teddington, Middlesex

Trouble at the top

SIR – Boris Johnson is being urged to get a grip and take control in the self-created turbulence he is experiencing. I suggest that shock tactics are needed; borrowing a hairbrush from Carrie and making a quick visit to his tailor for a decent well-fitting suit could be all it takes.

Tim Lovett
Claygate, Surrey

SIR – Another baby at No 10. Is the Prime Minister revealing his long-term strategy for staying in office by simply producing all the extra voters himself? A sure sign would be if he proposes a motion to lower the age for voting to 18 months. Additional evidence would

be if he has Cabinet support to allow ballot papers
to be filled in using coloured crayons.

Russ King
London N11

SIR – In today's political sketch Tim Stanley suggests
that Boris wants the No 10 garden to have a treehouse
not for the children but for himself. He asks us to
imagine him sitting up there with a pile of *Beanos*.
All very believable. He then suggests a sign on the
door: "No girlz allowed". I would suggest that Boris
is the least likely PM to ever demand such a thing.
Mr Stanley needs to work harder to place his sketches
more firmly in the believable sphere.

Matt Bentley
Stoke-on-Trent, Staffordshire

SIR – Sometimes when I can't sleep I dip into a book
entitled *Great British Wit*, published in 2005.
    What am I to make of the following entries
attributed to Boris Johnson?
    "There's as much chance of my becoming Prime
Minister as there is of finding Elvis on Mars, or
my being decapitated by a frisbee or reincarnated
as an olive."
    And: "My friends, as I have discovered myself,
there are no disasters, only opportunities. And,
indeed, opportunities for fresh disasters."

Vivien Womersley
Bath, Somerset

Wake me when he's gone

SIR – Last week I successfully underwent six hours of neurosurgery. When I woke I was asked if I knew who the Prime Minister was.

I was disappointed to learn that I supplied the correct answer.

Dr Timothy Davey
Bristol

SIR – Boris Johnson may not be the worst Prime Minister that this country has ever had, but it is certainly a position for which he is vying.

H. D. McCormack
Didcot, Oxfordshire

SIR – I think it would be helpful if you could publish an article reporting on the promises Boris Johnson has kept since he became Prime Minister, I have my suspicions that it will not require too much newsprint.

David Robertson
Basingstoke, Hampshire

SIR – Oh for the days when the naughtiest thing that the PM ever did was skip through a wheatfield!

Andrew Lutter
Newbury, Berkshire

SIR — I find myself so disgusted with the perpetually disingenuous performance of the Prime Minister that I'm afraid I may have no alternative but to relocate to Tunbridge Wells.

Christopher Banks
Edlesborough, Buckinghamshire

SIR — For some reason I keep seeing him stuck on that zip wire.

William Rusbridge
Tregony, Cornwall

SIR — Jeremy Hunt looks more prime ministerial by the minute. Aided by the fact that the bar is not set particularly high.

Dr Catherine Moloney
Liverpool

SIR — If Jeremy Hunt is the answer, we are asking the wrong question.

Nigel Adams
Hertford

SIR — My bus was late yesterday. Was this Boris Johnson's fault?
   He seems to get the blame for everything.

Peter Smith
Winchester, Hampshire

SIR – It transpires that Joe Biden and Boris Johnson have at least one thing in common – they're both doing their utmost to return their opponents to office.

Paul Greenwood
London N10

SIR – Donnez Boris Johnson un break. He is governing to the best of his wife's ability.

David Saunders
Sidmouth, Devon

It's that man again

SIR – Now that the local elections have delivered a resounding answer – "we don't want any of them" – is this not the time to put on the Spaghetti Western music and let the tumbleweed roll down the high street, ready for the return of Sheriff Tony and New, New Labour?

Peter Boxall
Haddenham, Buckinghamshire

SIR – When John Major lost the 1997 election and resigned as leader of the Conservatives, he famously said, "When the curtain falls it is time to get off the stage." I didn't catch what followed but presumably it was "…In order to heckle my successor(s), especially when they're abroad seeking (however ineptly) to address what is probably the biggest threat to world peace since 1945."

Andrew C. Pierce
Barnstaple, Devon

SIR – Does anyone really care what Sir John Major thinks about anything – other of course than Sir John Major?

Brian Goldthorpe
Harrogate, West Yorkshire

SIR – Ex-prime ministers, of all parties, should maintain a dignified silence.

Martin Moyes
Holt, Wiltshire

Playground politics

SIR – I see a cross-party committee has concluded that Members of Parliament should not be allowed to bring babies into the House of Commons chamber.

I have this image in my mind of a babe in arms being held by his mother during a debate suddenly shouting: "Point of Order, Mr Speaker!"

Dave Bassett
Liverpool

SIR — Whingeing and yelling, lying along the benches, falling asleep at random moments, interrupting important proceedings with outbursts of indecipherable nonsense, and gurgling with delight at the sight of a bare breast during a debate have no place in Parliament.

Babies, however, shouldn't be a problem.

> **Kevin Eyles**
> Blackburn, Lancashire

Great British food fight

SIR — The egging of Margaret Thatcher's statue in Grantham is a testament to the extraordinary woman and influential politician she was. The only person with egg on his face is the self-demeaning little man who threw it.

> **Felicity Thomson**
> Symington, Ayrshire

SIR — Amid these troubled times, should we be comforted to see that a university arts centre director appears to be so well paid that he can afford to throw expensive free-range eggs at a statue of Margaret Thatcher?

> **Clare Byam-Cook**
> London SW15

SIR — Boris Johnson wants farmers to "grow for Britain" in order to help ease the cost of living crisis.

I first became aware of the present Prime Minister's depth of agricultural knowledge during his campaign for leadership. A picture appeared in your paper taken at a farm just a couple of miles from here. It showed him trying to feed a group of cows in summertime, offering them sheep nuts. Strangely, they were ignoring him.

Peter McCabe
Milnthorpe, Cumbria

Looking for tractors

SIR – Neil Parish, who has resigned as an MP after he admitted watching pornography on his phone in the Commons, said he was initially looking for tractors. Given that he was once a farmer and chairman of the Environment, Food and Rural Affairs Committee, and that Escorts is a well-known brand of tractors, this is not as far-fetched as it may appear. MPs using their phones in the chamber to look for chicken breast recipes should be wary of clicking on any links.

David Miller
Chigwell, Essex

SIR – In light of recent events, I am re-reading *A Short History of Tractors in Ukrainian* by Marina Lewycka.

Janet Cook
York

SIR – We have recently had problems with mice, so I Googled "rent a cat".

This was not successful. A fine website appeared about a company based in Hayes from whom I could rent Caterpillar tractors. Not wishing to give up, I Googled "rent a pussycat". Another fine website came up, displaying the offerings of an enterprise in Soho. I think the MP for Tiverton and Honiton had bad luck. It could happen to anyone.

Edmund Sixsmith
London W6

SIR – My husband, aged 83, regularly searches for tractors online (we already have two). Should I be concerned?

Tessa Franklin
Kilve, Somerset

SIR – Several years ago I wanted to purchase a new large water container for the garden and made the mistake of Googling "large butts".

Coline Grover
Ross-on-Wye, Herefordshire

SIR – How on Earth did MPs manage in the House of Commons before mobile phones? I suppose those who weren't asleep were either reading the *Telegraph* or looking at page three of the tabloids.

Charlotte MacKay
Shaftesbury, Dorset

Now that the party's over

SIR – Criticism of Boris Johnson's administration for being shambolic is excessively harsh. They manifestly are capable of organising a booze-up in a brewery – or indeed almost anywhere else.

Edward Hill
Chandlers Ford, Hampshire

SIR – Apart from its use as a party venue, with a pied-à-terre for the Prime Minister to display his favourite domestic designs, what other function does 10 Downing Street currently serve in the great scheme of things?

Ian R. Lowry
Reading, Berkshire

SIR – We are informed that staff levels at No 10 in Margaret Thatcher's time were less than a tenth of what they are today.

Their booze-ups must have been rather dull.

Kenneth Preston
Royal Hillsborough, County Down

SIR – It would be ironic if an Abba party proved to be Boris Johnson's Waterloo.

Dr Eric Somerville
Wisbech, Cambridgeshire

SIR – The term "political party" has taken on a whole new meaning.

Jules Sanders
Weaverham, Cheshire

SIR – You know things are serious when Matt brings out "the man on the rack" in his cartoon.

John Brocklehurst
Weston under Wetherley, Warwickshire

Caution! Work in progress

SIR – If cheese and wine is an acceptable part of senior government meetings, I can begin to understand why so many resulting policies are incoherent.

Andrew Potter
Hartfield, East Sussex

SIR – I have this afternoon emailed my line manager requesting permission to bring a bottle of my choice to our next team meeting. Anything to relieve the boredom of work. I await her response with much anticipation.

Alan James
Nesscliffe, Shropshire

SIR – I am staggered to read that a suitcase was trundled into the local Co-op to be loaded with provisions, both wet and dry, for one Downing Street gathering.

I hold back no criticism whatsoever about donating to Labour Party funds. There is a perfectly fine Tesco store in the vicinity, the patronage of which would be more in line with Conservative Party ethos and the entrepreneurial spirit of "pile it high, sell it cheap", which was founder Jack Cohen's rallying cry.

John H. Lowe
Rossendale, Lancashire

SIR – We are looking forward to the publication of the No 10 Partygate canapé recipe book.

Lt Col Charles Carter (retd)
Llanteg, Pembrokeshire

SIR – I don't know about some people, but my idea of a party isn't a glass of mediocre wine and a slice of birthday cake with the boss.

Sandra Crawley
Shanklin, Isle of Wight

SIR – My daughters, who are now in their twenties, used to say it was not a party until the police were called.

Nik Perfitt
Bristol

SIR – The conjugation relating to get-togethers during Covid is as follows:

I attended a work meeting.

You attended a gathering.

He attended a party.

Barrie Bain
Wadhurst, East Sussex

SIR – The photograph of Sir Keir Starmer at a party is just how I imagined it would be. I expect most of Labour's local party workers were invited but decided being locked down would be more fun.

Keith Newman
Smarden, Kent

SIR – Is the answer to the question "When is a party not a party?" now: "When it's the Labour Party"?

Kip Calderara
Chesham, Buckinghamshire

SIR – You report that up to 75 per cent of civil servants are still working from home.

Perhaps we should congratulate the Prime Minister and Downing Street staff for actually being at their place of work, albeit with some drinks and refreshments to console them.

Judith Elborn
Hatfield, Hampshire

SIR – As there now appears to be a shortage of advisers, I would like to apply for the job. As I am a pensioner, the salary would come in handy. I believe I have more common sense than most of the current, recently resigned crop – and I am always happy to have a glass of wine and a piece of cake.

Amanda Dingle
Swindon, Wiltshire

Touch of Gray

SIR – How ironic that Sue Gray, the civil servant tasked with investigating Partygate, used to run a pub.

Mary Dennis
Faversham, Kent

SIR – Will the long-awaited report on the Downing Street parties be called "Fifty Shades of Gray"?

Simon McIlroy
Croydon, Surrey

SIR – With so little left to watch on Netflix, I think I will avoid reading Sue Gray's report and wait for the movie.

Richard Hodder
Four Elms, Kent

SIR – If Sue Gray's report is not published immediately and in full it won't be long before a copy is found in a London bus shelter or on a train.

Richard Snailham
Windsor, Berkshire

SIR – Godot never turned up.

Gareth Williams
Rockhampton, Gloucestershire

The verdict is in

SIR – I'm not wishing to downplay the events highlighted in Sue Gray's report. But if the SNP's Ian Blackford considers them to be "debauchery", then he needs to get out more.

Andrew Sturmey
Selby, North Yorkshire

SIR – The only people I've known to be "ambushed with a cake" were clowns in a circus.

Paul Norton
Derby

SIR – Never has a cake, eaten by so few, devastated so many.

S. Bullen
Thames Ditton, Surrey

SIR – If you can keep your job, when all about you are losing theirs, and blaming it on you, then you probably haven't accepted full responsibility for your actions after all.

> **Neil Truelove**
> Clifton, Bedfordshire

SIR – A friend tells me that, in the current context, "BYOB" stands for "Best you're off, Boris".

> **Roger Little**
> Tisbury, Wiltshire

SIR – I admire Sir Keir Starmer's moral stance in stating that he will resign if he is fined for breaking lockdown rules. I'm sure his statement had nothing whatsoever to do with Durham Police's stated policy of not issuing retrospective fines.

> **Alisdair Low**
> Richmond, Surrey

SIR – Drink beer, you're cleared; drink wine, you're fined.

> **Timothy Sharp**
> Duns, Berwickshire

SIR – BJ: "I will if you do."
    KS: "I'm not going to."
    BJ: "Well then, nor will I."
    BJ: "Who paid for the curry?"
    KS: "Who bought your wallpaper?"
Let's call the whole thing off…

Richard Kemm
Marseillan, Occitanie, France

"We're going to bash on"

SIR – As a supporter of the Labour Party I congratulate Boris on his victory in the vote of no confidence, and his determination not to resign.

Julian Badenoch
Cowes, Isle of Wight

SIR – The Prime Minister has said that it would take a flame-thrower to get him to leave office.

Perhaps then he is regretting the sale of the water cannon that he bought while mayor of London, just in case he needs it in the near future.

Jonathan T. R. Silverman
London NW2

SIR – The saddest news in the last week is not that Lord Geidt has resigned, but that Boris had an ethics adviser.

Ian Brent-Smith
Stratton Audley, Oxfordshire

SIR – I sincerely hope that Lord Geidt was not remunerated on the basis of results.

John Wright
Kirkella, East Yorkshire

SIR – Thank goodness Boris Johnson now admits he had heard the rumours about the disgraced deputy chief whip Chris Pincher. I was beginning to wonder if he had lost the journalistic instinct he might one day need to use again.

Roy Corlett
Southport, Lancashire

SIR – If I hear the phrase "getting on with the job" once more, I shall go the whole hog and vote Lib Dem next time around.

Howard March
Birmingham

Vanishing cabinet

SIR – At last: slimmed-down government. Perhaps Mr Johnson should take a lead from W. S. Gilbert and create a Minister of Everything Else.

Charles Penfold
Ulverston, Cumbria

SIR – Only Michael Gove could get himself sacked at the same time that everyone else is resigning.

> **David Lovie**
> Barrow upon Trent, Derbyshire

SIR – We have a new Chancellor in Nadhim Zahawi.

I doubt there would have been many applications for the position of purser AFTER the *Titanic* had hit the iceberg.

> **Ross Ellens**
> Milton Keynes, Buckinghamshire

SIR – Steve Barclay may look the part, but Boris Johnson missed a trick when he appointed him Health Secretary following Sajid Javid's resignation. George Clooney, with his great bedside manner and seven years' experience in ER, would really have motivated NHS staff.

> **Don Edwards**
> Lawford, Essex

SIR – According to *The Daily Telegraph*, "[Grant] Shapps has told Sky News that he is going nowhere." Is this because of the ongoing rail strikes under his watch as Transport Secretary?

> **Don Hamilton**
> York

SIR – I'm waiting to see what Dilyn does.

> **Roger Woodhouse**
> Twickenham, Middlesex

SIR – The most disappointing thing about education minister Andrea Jenkyns' rude gesture to the unfriendly crowds outside Downing Street is that it was not that traditional British riposte in such circumstances, the "V" sign.

Martin Coakley
Liphook, Hampshire

SIR – In this time of turmoil, who exactly is running the country?

Patricia Essex
Hedge End, Hampshire

Leave means leave

SIR – My dog has had a toy in the form of a clown for the last three years. We christened this toy "Boris".

Last evening the dog bit its head off and pulled all the stuffing out.

Graham Saunders
Winslow, Buckinghamshire

SIR – What next for Boris Johnson?

Perhaps the National Theatre could be persuaded to revive Alan Bennett's adaptation of *The Wind in the Willows*, where Boris could then play the most psychologically authentic Mr Toad anyone has seen.

Andrew Rissik
Stourport-on-Severn, Worcestershire

SIR – Now that Stanley Johnson has become a French citizen, I would suggest that his son Boris moves permanently to France to support his father. The benefits are obvious, not least that it would annoy the French.

Don Buchanan
Surbiton, Surrey

SIR – I so miss Boris; he brought such a sense of knowledge and calm dignity to proceedings.
   Wimbledon is just not the same without him.

Nick Symondson
Cheltenham, Gloucestershire

SIR – FOR SALE: POISONED CHALICE – APPLY NO 10 DOWNING STREET.

Michael Luckin
Chelmsford, Essex

Time for a fresh start

SIR – The next prime minister should be like my local laundrette, which is named Clean N Dry.

Stephen Havill
Torquay, Devon

SIR – As a Conservative Party member I will not be voting for any candidate seen out jogging.

Phil Angell
Helston, Cornwall

SIR – I suggest two qualifications for candidature:

1. Must not have been a member of the incumbent's Cabinet (more junior ministers may apply).

2. Must not be Jeremy Hunt.

Andrew C. Pierce
Barnstaple, Devon

SIR – Anyone thinking of putting themselves forward for prime minister should remember they'll have to live with Carrie's decor.

Cynthia Harrod-Eagles
Northwood, Middlesex

SIR – When the present occupants vacate the No 10 Downing Street flat, it would be an ideal opportunity to overpaint all the interior walls with magnolia emulsion.

This would then act as a reminder for future prime ministers that the public does not look favourably on any politicians' self-indulgence or profligacy, particularly at taxpayers' expense.

Hillary Bagshaw
Portsmouth, Hampshire

SIR – Has the new James Webb space telescope got a lens sharp enough to help the ordinary voter distinguish between those economic policies that are down to earth and those that are just pie in the sky?

Martin Henry
Good Easter, Essex

SIR – I note that, following genetic modification, the Magic Money Tree now flourishes in more southerly climes.

Richard Booth
Ringmer, East Sussex

SIR – As the leadership election commences, doggerel may offer an aside:

> *A party, Conservative in name alone,*
> *Has much for which it should atone.*
> *Politicians claim they wish to serve*
> *But display the "calibre" we deserve.*
> *I have the honour to be...*

Andrew Newcombe QC
Combe Down, Somerset

Whatsit, So-and-so and Thingummy

SIR – When the Conservative Government of 1852 was formed by Lord Derby it was filled with so many lightweight figures that it survived only eight months and is forever called the "Who? Who?" ministry.

Looking at the contenders for the present post, I am inclined to think that history may repeat itself in terms of obscurity and duration.

Dorian Wood
Castle Cary, Somerset

SIR – Surely the time has come for a new Bateman cartoon: "The Tory MP NOT standing for the leadership of the Party."

Michael Brotherton
Chippenham, Wiltshire

SIR – If one were to name the most memorable prime ministers since the war, excluding Churchill, one might say Harold Macmillan, Margaret Thatcher, Tony Blair and Boris Johnson. What is noticeable is that they come to power roughly every 20 years. I suppose we now have to wait until 2040 for the next one.

Brian Cole
Robertsbridge, East Sussex

SIR – I really think they ought to include a "none of the above" option on the ballot paper. It might even come out top.

John Godfrey
Hitchin, Hertfordshire

And in this corner...

SIR – The demise of Boris Johnson was warmly received by many in anticipation of a replacement who can restore faith and integrity within the Conservative Party. This warm wave of excitement quickly disappeared when Liz Truss announced she had thrown her hat into the ring.

Chris Learmont-Hughes
Caldy, Wirral

SIR – Going by her calm demeanour while being attacked by members of her own party, I'd say Penny Mordaunt may well have been sawn in two when she was a magician's assistant – which gives her the edge when it comes to the cut and thrust of this leadership election.

Chris Fitzpatrick
Dublin, Ireland

SIR – If we are to have a new, male prime minister, could we at least have one whose trousers have been introduced to his shoes?

Simon Baumgartner
East Molesey, Surrey

SIR – Jacket and tie, immaculate hair, direct talk, military background, good sense of humour, no previous convictions. Tom Tugendhat for prime minister.

James Service
Ludlow, Shropshire

SIR – As a young man I used to breed and show Gloster canaries in Gloucester. The older members of our society were always generous with their pearls of wisdom.

The verdict was that in competitions, a good "little un" will beat a poor "big un", but a good "big un" will always beat a good "little un". All things being equal, the electorate will usually vote for the one with the "big hair".

Over the years, these wisdoms have usually proven to be correct. Take note, politicians.

Francis Bongiovanni
Cheltenham, Gloucestershire

SIR — Newspaper headline writers only hope that whoever wins has a short name.

Arthur W. J. G. Ord-Hume
Guildford, Surrey

SIR — I am thoroughly bored by this whole process. Why not just put names in a hat?

Judith Barnes
St Ives, Cambridgeshire

The right stuff

SIR — I was surprised but encouraged to learn that there is a Common Sense Group of Conservative MPs under the chairmanship of Sir John Hayes. I presume that this is a very new group.

I suggest that they take over government until the new leader is installed — or even beyond that.

Stewart Harper
Burstow, Surrey

SIR – Since Larry the cat is going to stay at No 10, perhaps he should decide who he wants to share his home with. The candidates would gather and wait to see whose lap he chooses to sit on. Anyone found to be offering a bribe in the form of cat treats or toys would be disqualified.

It is as good a method of selection as any other, and much quicker.

Anne Harvey
Seaford, East Sussex

SIR – I think Larry should be prime minister. He's been resident at No 10 for a long time, knows the ropes and hasn't put a paw wrong. He has never been found negligent of his mouse-catching duties – plus, he's always beautifully groomed.

Karen Réné
Leicester

SIR – If we are to have a meaningful change in government, then I suggest the following:
Prime Minister: Allison Pearson
Chancellor: Roger Bootle
Home Secretary: Michael Deacon
Foreign Secretary: Matt

Fred Wilson
Newcastle upon Tyne

SIR – There are many problems at home and around the world today, but all these problems could be resolved in one fell swoop if the Telegraph Letter-Writers Party were to be given control. Except, of course, the debate on the consumption of marmalade.

Owen Hay
Colchester, Essex

SIR – I propose that the current Cabinet is replaced by the skilful, diligent and delightful specialists from *The Repair Shop*. They represent so much of what is still splendid about this country. Confidence will be restored immediately and we will be the envy of the world.

Alasdair Ogilvy
Stedham, West Sussex

Europe cut off

SIR – I wonder if Boris Johnson has any idea how many potential voters he loses every time he refers to "Our friends in Brussels".

He appears to be the only person in Britain who doesn't realise that we have no friends in Brussels.

Peter J. Robinson
Lichfield, Staffordshire

SIR – Does the news that Jacob Rees-Mogg, the so-called "Honourable Member for the 18th Century", has been appointed Minister for Brexit Opportunities, mean war with France?

Dr Tim Brooks
London E11

SIR – Jacob Rees-Mogg is minister for the opportunities offered by Brexit. I hope that as a first step he will explain to us all what they are.

Dick Russell
Beenham, Berkshire

SIR – Brexit could have been achieved so much more simply and to mutual satisfaction by agreeing to pay the EU's opening demand for 100 billion euros on the sole condition that a French waiter was put in charge of collecting the money.

Edward Hill
Chandlers Ford, Hampshire

SIR – In 5,000 million years, the Sun will expand and engulf the Earth. This will be a direct consequence of Brexit.

Adam Massingham
Ashford, Kent

The Scottish question

SIR – Pro-independence supporters in Scotland have already started their campaign, with "Yes" featuring on banners and posters. Supposing they are right that there will be a referendum, how do they know what the question will be? It could be: "Do you wish to remain in the United Kingdom?"

Now, that would be fun.

Nigel Johnson-Hill
Petersfield, Hampshire

SIR – The Scottish independence referendum was touted by the SNP as a once-in-a-lifetime opportunity.

Perhaps Scotland's First Minister, Nicola Sturgeon, might be so kind and tell us which calendar she is using that defines "a lifetime" as a period of approximately eight years.

Brian Weatherley
Salisbury, Wiltshire

SIR – Nicola Sturgeon is seriously missing a trick if she excludes the English from voting in her proposed second referendum.

Gillian Grant
Bude, Cornwall

SIR – I'm pleased to see that the First Minister has absolutely no other worries of any consequence in her in-tray.

Simon Morpuss
Stratford-upon-Avon, Warwickshire

Thinning blue line

SIR – Yesterday morning, I spotted a policeman on foot in our town centre.

In the afternoon, I saw a police car.

Is this double sighting unusual for this time of year?

Howard Stevens
Stockton-on-Tees, Co Durham

SIR – Andy Cooke, the new Chief Inspector of Constabulary, says the police "are not the thought police".

In light of his advice to officers to use discretion when dealing with shoplifters, it would appear that the police are not even the police anymore.

Stefan Badham
Portsmouth, Hampshire

SIR – There are 358,076 criminal cases waiting to be heard in the few remaining magistrates' courts in this country. It's just as well that hardly any burglars are being caught.

Dr Richard Soper
Bury St Edmunds, Suffolk

SIR – Perhaps the quality of life of detectives working from home could be enhanced even further if burglars could be persuaded to do the same.

Richard Watson
Formby, Lancashire

SIR – I thought community payback meant completing a number of hours of unpaid work for the benefit of the local community. This could include litter picking and graffiti removal. The offenders concerned would set their alarm clocks for an early start, don a hi-vis vest, fill a Thermos and pack a Spam sandwich in readiness for a hard day's toil.

How wrong could I have been? Instead of the alarm, Thermos and sandwich, now it's a lie-in, fry-up and a pot of tea. At around ten o'clock, the cardboard, crayons, glitter and felt-tip pens come out for a couple of hours of card-making.

Maybe they'll make "Sorry I Stole Your Jewellery" cards (using rhinestones of course and not the diamonds from your tiara).

Gary Freestone
Leicester

SIR – Police in Gloucestershire have failed to track down a stolen teddy bear. I am no detective, but if they went down in the woods today, they would be sure of a big surprise.

Terry Reeves
Coventry, Warwickshire

SIR – I suggest that Commissioner Selwyn Patterson from *Death in Paradise* would make an ideal replacement for Cressida Dick, the outgoing head of the Metropolitan Police.

He has a 100 per cent crime clean-up rate and could bring his excellent support team with him.

Andrew Jones
Hertford

SIR – I wonder if the Mayor of London, Sadiq Khan, has ever considered losing confidence in himself.

Chandos Monro
Winchester, Hampshire

Papers, please

SIR – After weeks of searching I have finally found my passport. It was in a much-searched drawer with my expired passports and, like them, had a piece of paper stuck across the front. It was only when I looked closer and peeled the paper off that I realised it was part of a luggage tag.

I now have a certain sympathy for the brain-fogged inefficiency of the Passport Office. There are a lot of us about.

> **Lesley Thompson**
> Lavenham, Suffolk

SIR – Perhaps George Bernard Shaw's famous maxim should be updated: "He who can, does. He who cannot, works in the public sector."

> **David McFetrich**
> Poole, Dorset

SIR – Delays, excuses, no out-of-hours access, hurdles to jump before you can be seen – have GPs been awarded the contract for processing Ukrainian refugees?

> **Victor Launert**
> Matlock Bath, Derbyshire

SIR – Just as no battle plan survives contact with the enemy, it seems no ministerial initiative survives contact with a Home Office civil servant.

> **Stephen Garner**
> Colchester, Essex

SIR – I wonder if the staff of the Home Office are taking the name of the department they work for too literally.

> **Judith Anthony**
> Exmouth, Devon

SIR – Before I went to work as a part-time civil servant I had always regarded *Yes Minister* as a good comedy. Only after I started work there did I realise it was in fact a documentary.

Ian Wallace
Whitley Bay, Northumberland

SIR – Where do the Civil Service and social workers store all the lessons that they learn?

Robert Dows-Miller
Escrick, Yorkshire

SIR – The Government wants us to take Ukrainian refugees into our homes. It would be a very fine gesture to make Chequers, Chevening and Dorneywood available.

Andrew Dyke
London N21

SIR – I read that civil servants are in "open rebellion" over the Government's plan to send illegal immigrants to Rwanda for processing, and that they are threatening "mass walkouts".

As most of them are still working from home, does it mean they will be walking out of their spare bedrooms?

Steve Narancic
Wantage, Oxfordshire

SIR – To all those civil servants who can't get flights to their villas in France, Spain or Italy: apologies from the airlines, but the flight crews are now working from home.

M. Burbidge
Bexhill, East Sussex

SIR – If it is up to civil servants to decide how they work (or not), then surely it can be up to me to decide how I pay their salaries... sorry, I mean my tax.

Alison Thomas
Leatherhead, Surrey

SIR – Hybrid vigour is a recognised requirement for a healthy plant or animal.

Over breakfast yesterday, I wondered if this principle could in any way be applicable to recent criticism of our Civil Service.

A rapid review of the alma mater of the permanent secretaries on the Civil Service Board produced the following: University of Oxford, 5. University of Cambridge, 3. Others, 2.

Over time such a small gene pool would, in plant breeding circles, produce misshapen tomatoes and in farming, five-legged sheep.

I had a second cup of coffee and wondered if my comparison had been taken too far.

Anthony Collins FRCP
Totnes, Devon

Little green men

SIR – Our tumble dryer, which we do our best to ignore, is called – coincidentally – Greta, like the preachy Scandinavian who spread virtue at Glastonbury. Our tumble dryer goes round and round and round, is going nowhere, generates hot air and will one day inevitably leave us with an enormous bill.

Charles Foster
Chalfont St Peter, Buckinghamshire

SIR – Next year the Glastonbury Festival should only be on a virtual basis. This will do much to help the environment and will also save the BBC a bob or two.

Julian Goulding
Reigate, Surrey

SIR – Extinction Rebellion's only goal is to make everyone else as unproductive as they are.

Paul Gaynor
Windermere, Cumbria

SIR – It is most heartening that British innovation has developed a method for collecting the space junk in orbit around our planet. Let's hope the boffins can build on this technological advance and develop a machine that captures Earth-bound litter louts and relocates them to outer space. Now that would truly be progress.

Dr Howard A. Bell
Brough, Cumbria

SIR – Yesterday, aliens from a far-off civilisation visited Earth on a reconnaissance mission.

They reported back to their government that they found no signs of intelligent life.

John Catchpole
Beverley, East Yorkshire

So that went well…

SIR – In March 2021 I wrote to you wondering what I could possibly renounce for Lent after the first year of Covid had denied me many pleasures. Twelve months later I thought the choice was going to be easy. I would give up worrying.

Fat chance!

Alan Frost
Bournemouth, Dorset

SIR – We have been feeding an abandoned cat, who is so terrified that he will only come indoors for something to eat if the door is left open to provide an escape route. Although I feel very sorry for him, at least he has never heard of Vladimir Putin or climate change.

Brian Christley
Abergele, Conwy

SIR – We are all aware of July and August being the "silly season" in the media, but I suggest that this year we adopt the alternative of "very stupid season".

No political bias here.

John Breining-Riches
Chagford, Devon

SIR – Is there a collective noun for "unprecedented crises"? There do seem to be a lot of them about.

Paul Fairweather
Henley-on-Thames, Oxfordshire

SIR – How I long to live in precedented times.

Julia Sharpe
Salisbury, Wiltshire

HOME
THOUGHTS ON
ABROAD

Sorry states

SIR – When Egyptians placed a pharaoh in a pyramid, they removed their brains.

The Americans seem to do something similar when they place someone in the White House.

John Kennedy
Hornchurch, Essex

SIR – The answer to gun crime in America lies not in the number of guns there are but in the price of bullets. Tax bullets so that each one costs $500 and gun crime will plummet.

Jeremy Dearling
King's Lynn, Norfolk

SIR – It may be helpful to examine the actual text of the US Second Amendment: "A well regulated Militia, being necessary to the security of a free State, the right of the people to keep and bear Arms, shall not be infringed."

Salvador Ramos, the school shooter who murdered 21 people (19 of them children), was not a member of a citizen militia, well regulated or otherwise. I also suggest that the last time a well-regulated militia served any useful function of public protection was in the 1860s.

Anthony Pick
Newbury, Berkshire

SIR – Modern American women seeking to overturn the ruling by the Supreme Court on Roe vs Wade seem to lack a classical education. Aristophanes demonstrated in his play *Lysistrata* that the way to stop men making silly laws is to refuse to sleep with them. It usually works.

> J. W.
> Via email

Entente none too cordiale

SIR – The French president Emmanuel Macron is suggesting that Britain could possibly join the EU's "outer ring". Clearly, his bedtime reading has been Dante's *Inferno*. Does he envisage Britain doomed to spend eternity in the sixth circle (heresy) or the ninth circle (treachery)?

> **Duncan McAra**
> Bishopbriggs, East Dunbartonshire

SIR – Do any of your readers know how long the O-Macron variant is likely to remain toxic?

> **William Hunter**
> Midhurst, West Sussex

SIR – What is the French word for "jumped-up"?

> **James Hargan**
> Dronfield, Derbyshire

SIR – President Macron is keen on preserving "*une bretelle de sortie*" for Russia's Vladimir Putin to extract himself from his Ukrainian disaster. I suggest that he offers up the French Government-owned property of Longwood House, which has a venerable history of accommodating a notorious international statesman in the past.

Putin enjoys billiards and the property boasts a fine billiard room. Putin would also enjoy the excellent game fishing that is available on St Helena.

Chris Butler
Borough Green, Kent

The Russian bear moves in

SIR – President Vladimir Putin has denied any threat to Ukraine.

"It is just a friendly gathering of Russian troops on the border", said a spokesman.

John Catchpole
Beverley, East Yorkshire

SIR – Russia has reduced troop numbers at the Ukrainian border. Both soldiers are now back in Moscow.

Ray Rees
Llanelli, Carmarthenshire

SIR – My wife and I were clearing out some drawers and found a copy of *The Daily Telegraph*. Our attention was drawn to an article headed: "Ukraine and Moscow, Friendship not too cordial". Nothing too odd there perhaps, but the date? 10 July 1928.

Chris Burvill
Crowborough, East Sussex

SIR – President Putin is suffering from a condition known as "End of Empire". Great Britain suffered the same in the 1960s. If he is sensible, then he will recover in due course.

Michael Reading
Ash, Surrey

SIR – Mr Putin should be reminded that hubris is generally followed by nemesis.

Colin Streeter
Fletching, East Sussex

SIR – Students at the Army Staff College before the fall of the Berlin Wall will doubtless remember the joke poster, ostensibly for the Russian airline Aeroflot, which was used to introduce Warsaw Pact studies. Instead of an attractive air stewardess there was a grim-visaged Russian army officer above a caption which read: "Visit Mother Russia – Before She Visits You".

Lt Col Christopher Sharp (retd)
Kenilworth, Warwickshire

SIR – My mother-in-law had a saying: "Who gets more wants more". Beware Putin.

Alan Hollowood
Blandford Forum, Dorset

SIR – I note that the Duma has passed a law threatening 15 years' imprisonment for anyone propagating "fake" news about Russian military operations. Which prosecutor will be brave enough to indict Putin?

Robin Goodfellow
Hersham, Surrey

SIR – The Russian Government reminds me of Blackadder. "Deny everything, Baldrick!"

Jenny Arnold
Kingsbridge, Devon

SIR – In view of Mr Putin's sensitivity to certain words and my fear of a 15-year prison sentence, I have now retitled my copy of Tolstoy's great work *Special Military Operation and Peace*.

Dennis Rolfe
London NW3

SIR – The Russian troops are indeed peacekeepers. The concern is how many pieces they want to keep.

Uri Scelwyn
Collingbourne Ducis, Wiltshire

SIR – Watching the military parade through Moscow's Red Square, I wonder what percentage of the Russian GDP is spent on medals.

Graeme Wright
Sutton Coldfield, West Midlands

The Western front

SIR – 1939: Germany invades Poland. The UK declares war on Germany.

2022: Russia invades Ukraine. The UK says, "Naughty, naughty, no pocket money for you, then!"

Andrew F. Drummond
Blandford Forum, Dorset

SIR – The nuclear deterrent certainly works. It has prevented the West from acting to prevent the invasion of Ukraine, a major refugee crisis and the destruction of towns and cities.

Peter Goldberger
Leeds, West Yorkshire

SIR – Now that all of the Western leaders have proved themselves to be utterly terrified of Putin, perhaps it's time they did something useful and learnt to speak fluent Russian.

At least, that way, they could collaborate with him in his own language.

Liam Power
Dundalk, Co Louth, Ireland

SIR – Mr Putin has certainly cost the West a lot of travel expenses.

Rene Schurtenberger
Seer Green, Buckinghamshire

SIR – It is just 10 years since the EU won the Nobel Peace Prize. Given recent events, are there plans to give it back?

Kathleen Dunmore
Nottingham

SIR – It would be good if Italy impounded Putin's luxury yacht, painted it in Ukrainian colours and used it to re-home refugees.

June Abbott
Ventnor, Isle of Wight

SIR – I suggest that the Mayor of London changes the name of Kensington Palace Gardens to Free Ukraine.
  Then the Russian Embassy will have to give their address as 6/7 Free Ukraine, London W8 4QP.

Steve Cattell
Grantham, Lincolnshire

SIR – Vladimir Putin has described the imposition of sanctions against Russia as an act of war. Of course, it is no such thing. He may rest assured that they simply form part of a Special Economic Operation.

David Platts
Syerston, Nottinghamshire

That'll teach him

SIR – The Prime Minister may feel that his announced sanctions will prove a powerful threat. I am unfortunately reminded of *Yes, Prime Minister* and the Governor of the Bank of England, Sir Desmond Glazebrook, whose most feared weapon against serious offenders in the City of London was to have lunch with them.

Philip Brennan
Oxhill, Warwickshire

SIR – I have taken Vladimir Putin off of my Christmas card list. It will probably have as much effect as the official sanctions being imposed on him.

George Brown
Manchester

SIR – Could we not enlist the persuasive power of the Swedish activist Greta Thunberg to speak to Putin to stop the massive advance of 10,000 NEVs (non-electric vehicles) into Ukraine? The carbon emissions of this fleet must be keeping her awake at night.

She seems to have the ear of every leader of the Western democratic world and could surely persuade Putin of the irreparable damage his attack on Ukraine is doing to the climate.

Colin T. Graham
Cheltenham, Gloucestershire

SIR – When I joined a visiting choir to Hereford this weekend, support for Ukraine was apparent in both the cathedral and in services. The new dean, Sarah Brown, led a prayer for rain in the intercessions, "to hinder the progress of advancing enemy tanks".

Nigel Kenyon
Windsor, Berkshire

SIR – I'm sure we are all grateful to the Bishop of Leeds for his moral guidance about how we should all accommodate Russia's unprovoked aggression in Ukraine.

Perhaps he should be invited to head an alternative to the criminal justice system which aims at avoiding stigmatising criminals by first asking them what they desire and then demanding that prospective victims concede part of their demands.

For example, if a psychopath declares a desire to kill an individual with a machete, then the arbiter could approve the hacking-off of one limb as a suitable compromise.

Kenneth Preston
Royal Hillsborough, Co Down

SIR – Having had to watch the Eurovision Song Contest at my wife's behest, I can see why Vladimir Putin has some anxiety about his country being surrounded by Europe. The fact that Australia, as well as Azerbaijan, Moldova and Ukraine are considered European enough to enter the contest has obviously given him food for thought. This supposed enlargement of Europe does not, or course, condone his actions at all.

Malcolm Freeth
Bournemouth, Dorset

SIR – Now that Russia has been banned from the Eurovision Song Contest, I think that President Putin must know that the West really means business. The Ukrainian people can heave a sigh of relief.

Jonathan Whybrow
Liss, Hampshire

SIR – I thought we were supposed to be punishing Russia, not rewarding it.

Hannah Hunt
Woodhall Spa, Lincolnshire

Ukraine takes a swipe

SIR – When I visited Kyiv in 2015, it was clear what the people of Ukraine really thought of Putin.

On market stalls all around the capital, and beyond, were piled great pyramids of patterned loo rolls.

The most popular design was the one with Putin's portrait printed on every sheet.

Veronica Timperley
London W1

SIR – Putting the Mayor of Kyiv, Vitali Klitschko, and Vladimir Putin in a boxing ring together would be one way of settling the Russia–Ukraine conflict. Putin wouldn't make it to the end of the first round.

David Williams
Nottingham

SIR – We must be thankful that the former comedian Volodymyr Zelensky is proving a better leader than our own joker.

Michael McGough
Loughton, Essex

SIR – Might it be possible to clone the spirited Ukrainian civil activist Daria Kaleniuk and have these clones replace the clowns presently occupying the House of Commons?

Nathan Hunt
Datchet, Berkshire

SIR – Vladimir Putin has blamed his decision to threaten the world with thermonuclear war on Liz Truss. It appears that the comedian was in the Kremlin all along.

R. W.
Via email

I see no ships

SIR – On the eve of what has the potential for
becoming a major world conflict, it is comforting to
know that our two largest capital ships, the aircraft
carriers HMS *Queen Elizabeth* and HMS *Prince of Wales*,
lie at anchor in their home port of Portsmouth
undergoing urgent repairs.

Jeremy Somers
Chipping Norton, Oxfordshire

SIR – The suggestion that Britain's pitifully
diminished Armed Forces could in any way influence
Russia's intentions as regards Ukraine is at best
laughable and at worst extremely naive and dangerous.

With successive governments reducing our land
forces to less than that required to constitute a militia,
we have no sabre to rattle – rather a small knife for
peeling fruit.

Simon Crowley
Kemsing, Kent

SIR – It is evident that the current security risk with
Russia does not come from tanks and boots on the
ground but cyber warfare.

Hopefully our security services have recruited a
posse of 16-year-olds to take on Putin from their
bedrooms.

Peter Le Patourel
Truro, Cornwall

SIR – When I was at Officer Cadet School in the 1950s we were told that if any of us ever aspired to higher command there were three things one should never do:
1. Get involved in the Balkans
2. Invade Afghanistan
3. March on Moscow
Having tried 1 and 2 I hope we are not about to try 3.

Tony Barron
Godalming, Surrey

SIR – I don't feel proud standing on the edge of the crowd looking in, holding the jacket for the little kid who's taking on the school bully in the playground.

Brian Galipeau
Looe, Cornwall

SIR – German Chancellor Olaf Scholz claims his country is sending more military weapons to Ukraine than Britain. Is he including broomsticks?

Dr R. D. Ogilvy
Nottingham

SIR – Ghost hunters may be interested to learn that anyone visiting the American military cemetery in Hamm, Luxembourg at midnight may hear the disembodied voice of General George S. Patton call, "I told you schmucks what the Russians would do the moment we disarmed even if they gave up Communism."

Mark Boyle
Johnstone, Renfrewshire

SIR – Cheer up – Gavin Williamson might still be our Secretary of State for Defence.

Dr Tony Parker
Ringmer, East Sussex

Vlad the invader

SIR – We hear again and again that no one wants to push Vladimir Putin over the edge – but he is over the edge by miles already.

Camilla Coats-Carr
Teddington, Middlesex

SIR – Peter the Great; Vladimir the Small.

Jonathan Higgins
Morden, Surrey

SIR – A clerihew for Putin:
Vladimir Putin
Likes putting the boot in
But is finding Ukraine
A bit of a pain

Geoff Neden
Diddlebury, Shropshire

SIR – Putin is well named. He should be put in prison, or put in the ground.

Pat Greenwood
Northallerton, North Yorkshire

SIR – Come back Mikhail Gorbachev, all is forgiven.

Peter Collings
Winchester, Hampshire

SIR – Congratulations to Mr Putin on passing his
screen test for the next Bond film. His latest meeting
at the Kremlin showed him as a definitive Dr Evil –
remote desk in an icy lair, quaking henchmen and
missing only the white cat.

Mike Arthur
Plymouth, Devon

SIR – Just in case any of President Putin's inner circle
at the Kremlin were prevaricating, now would be a
good time to loosen the stair carpet.

Joan Martin
Whitby, North Yorkshire

SIR – It has been suggested that President Putin is
suffering from "short man syndrome". I am 5ft 3in;
I have never invaded another country in my life and at
the age of 85 it is now unlikely that I will.

Peter Chilvers
Royston, Hertfordshire

SIR – The re-opening of former McDonald's
premises in Russia (under a new logo and name) has
seen the launch of Russia's answer to the Big Mac,
known as the McPutin.

Early diners have commented anonymously that the burger is much smaller than advertised, leaves a nasty taste in the mouth and does not give value for money.

David S. Ainsworth
Manchester

SIR – Hearing Vladimir Putin justify his war crimes by quoting from the Bible has strengthened my faith in agnosticism. I am, however, coming to believe in the devil.

Gareth Williams
Rockhampton, Gloucestershire

Russia's roulette

SIR – Fraser Nelson writes that Putin will live to regret the war.

Surely, the best chance of this disaster coming to an end is if he doesn't.

Robert Hurran
Amersham, Buckinghamshire

SIR – It must be time for MI6 to recall Agent Putin before he is assassinated. He has unified Ukraine and filled it with national pride, restored NATO solidarity, trashed the Russian economy, humiliated the Red Army and closed Russia down. No politician would do this to his country unless...

Martyn Thomas
Usk, Monmouthshire

SIR – Surely Vladimir Putin, like all world leaders, has *The Daily Telegraph* delivered to the Kremlin, or if not will have access to the digital edition. He should therefore have knowledge of how badly his "Special Operation" is going. If there is any doubt, why not give him a free subscription? A small but worthwhile gift.

Richard Hall
Great Missenden, Buckinghamshire

SIR – Saturday's Review section of *The Daily Telegraph* includes a synopsis for *Animal Farm*:

"A group of animals band together to overthrow their corrupt owner, and set up their own ideal farm, but this all disintegrates when a Stalinesque pig becomes power hungry."

On reflection I thought I would give this a miss and watch the news instead.

Peter Kievenaar
Chelsworth, Suffolk

TRAVELLING
HOPEFULLY

The open road

SIR – I thought I'd seen most things but on my way home on Sunday evening, near dusk, I overtook a cyclist wearing camouflage gear. At least I think I did.

> **Alan Mottram**
> Tarporley, Cheshire

SIR – My wife and I go for a walk along Worthing seafront at five in the morning. We often come across a young man cycling, no hands, dressed in black, smoking a joint and texting.

I have to say I quite admire his *joie de vivre*.

> **Tim Harmey**
> Worthing, West Sussex

SIR – Two sights yesterday convinced me that spring has arrived.

The first was a car with the roof down and a big shaggy dog sitting up on the back seat, wearing goggles. The second was a man pedalling a sit-up-and-beg bicycle along the Broad Walk in Kensington Gardens, wearing a cloth cap on which perched what looked like a raven. Every so often the man would take a bit of bread from his pocket and give it to the bird.

> **Roger Hudson**
> London W8

SIR – An elderly friend was in the habit of knocking his pipe out against the outside of the car door as he drove along.

On one journey he mistakenly thought a fog had reduced visibility. In fact it was his overcoat smouldering on the back seat from the effects of the hot pipe residue blown back into the car.

Vicky Postlethwaite
Fovant, Salisbury

SIR – I always wear a hat in my car, my excuse being it has no roof.

With uncanny reliability my hat will fly off at anything above the national speed limit. I suggest the practice has much to commend it.

Maxwell Blake
London SW3

SIR – When my husband sees the road sign for "uneven surface", he says, "Watch out, bras in the road".

He's still hopeful, even after almost 60 years of driving.

Judy Parsley
London W4

SIR – I wonder if it might be possible to train birds (vultures perhaps) to deliver parking tickets.

Having placed the penalty notice on the screen, trained birds would need little encouragement to leave a personal penalty of their own creation.

Nicholas Young
London W13

Britain hits the buffers

SIR – Thank you for the front-page photograph of Mick Lynch, the general secretary of the rail union RMT.

Every week I line the bottom of my kitchen wastebin with a used newspaper. I am sure I will derive as much pleasure from dropping rubbish on him as he does from inflicting misery on the public.

Tony Berry
Hertford

SIR – If you like the rail strike, you'll love a Labour Government.

Jim Dawes
Maidstone, Kent

SIR – I have finally realised what the letters RMT mean: Red Militant Trotskyites.

Francis Bown
London E3

SIR – The proposed rail strikes are a depressing echo of times past. However, it is reported that traffic wardens in parts of the country are also planning to strike, which I suspect may be greeted by the public with rather more enthusiasm.

Lovat Timbrell
Brighton, East Sussex

SIR – The rail strikes will provide certainty for passengers.

They won't turn up at the station expecting a train to arrive. Compare this to a non-strike day when they turn up and the train is cancelled.

Lisa Dumbavand
London SW18

SIR – I don't understand the controversy surrounding driverless trains.

We have a lot of driverless trains. The problem is that they are not moving.

Ian Mack
Via email

This project is a train wreck

SIR – Who needs Storms Malik and Corrie to flatten thousands of trees and uproot miles of hedgerow? HS2 does it all by itself every day.

Elizabeth Thame
Banbury, Oxfordshire

SIR – HS2 would make the perfect cycle track and really would please a lot of people.

Ron Burton
Bishopstoke, Hampshire

See it, say it, sorted

SIR – Whenever the train announcement asks passengers to make a report "if you see something that doesn't look right", my wife looks disconcertingly at me.

Anthony Gales
Henham, Essex

SIR – According to Transport for London's new posters, "intrusive staring of a sexual nature is sexual harassment and is not tolerated". People will be turning to the broadsheet of *The Daily Telegraph* in droves so that they can hide their eyes to protect reputations. Tabloids might not be sufficient.

Christopher Hunt
Swanley, Kent

SIR – If Sadiq Khan is worried about staring on the London Underground, how long will it be before blindfolds are mandatory on TfL?

Barry Mackenzie
Hoddesdon, Hertfordshire

Anywhere away from here

SIR – Andy Prendergast, the national secretary of the GMB union, has suggested that travelling abroad without checked baggage is "one less thing to worry about". However, for a completely stress-free long weekend, lying down in a darkened room can bring a wonderful tranquillity.

Cameron Morice
Reading, Berkshire

SIR – On holiday in Sicily with my grown-up children, I was sent to buy wine. As I considered the logistical issues involved in acquiring sufficient quantities to satisfy them, I remembered the technique developed by the team at 10 Downing Street. I can strongly recommend a small-wheeled travelling suitcase as the perfect way for transporting half a dozen or more wine bottles.

Nick Bell
Andover, Hampshire

SIR – While I understand the safety benefits of putting children in helmets while they are skiing, it has completely ruined the great old game of pulling off their bobble hats and throwing them to the back of the queue if they try to squeeze past.

Richard Sinnerton
(currently in a long queue at Font-Romeu)
Woking, Surrey

SIR — I flew British Airways long-haul last week. The purser informed us that there would be "zero tolerance" of anyone who refused to wear a mask. I pondered this conundrum as both I and the lady next to me were served our meals and proceeded to eat, maskless, within 30 inches of each other.

Alexander Williams
Kingston upon Thames, Surrey

SIR — In my time as a long-haul airline commander we used to stop in a five-star hotel in Narita, a town near Tokyo. In my bathroom were the customary accessories, including a hairdryer. On this was a card stating: "This Is For The Drying Of The Hair And Not For The Other Purpose". I never found out what that might have been. Any ideas?

Anthony McLauchlan
Piltdown, East Sussex

SIR — A graphic in Dubrovnik Airport warns not to put one's penis in the hand-drier. In my opinion a dose of Darwinian survival of the fittest may be good for humanity.

Dorian Wood
Castle Cary, Somerset

SIR — Can someone please tell me why, whenever I stay in a hotel room, the end of the loo roll has been folded neatly into a triangle?

Peter Harper
Salisbury, Wiltshire

SIR – My favourite single-fill sandwich has to be sanded beetroot on white eaten on Barry Island beach, usually in the rain.

Howard Thomas
Sandown, Isle of Wight

SIR – Back in the early 1980s the deckchair concession on Castle Beach in Tenby had a deckchair that had been altered, making it impossible to put up. This was reserved for the rudest, most aggressive male customer of the day. His wife would be given a normal deckchair and she could sit back and relax as he set about his unenviable task in front of an amused public.

Mark Brindley
Tenby, Pembrokeshire

GOOD AND
BAD SPORTS

Winter (Olympics) of our discontent

SIR — Are we watching the Winter Olympics or the Eurovision Song Contest?

"GB nul points".

Graham Barber
Sudbury, Suffolk

SIR — Why should anyone expect us to be any good at winter sports? It rarely snows and we have few facilities. We prefer gallant triers like Eddie the Eagle. Mind you, our curlers aren't bad, so we can always hope.

John Taylor
Purley, Greater London

SIR — Curling is a game, not a sport. More like shove ha'penny on ice, only on a bigger scale.

Paul Williams
Torquay, Devon

SIR — I am sure that despite the accolade all winners were disappointed with the bottom of a can of beans that they were given as a medal — spray-painted the appropriate colour, of course.

Sandy Callander
Bristol

SIR – The teenage figure skater Kamila Valieva has stated that she failed her drug test because of contamination via her grandfather's medication. It makes me wonder how many times the family dog has eaten her homework.

Dr M. G. Young
Salisbury, Wiltshire

SIR – If the International Olympic Committee is open to suggestions for a new sport for the 2024 Olympic Games in Paris, I suggest knitting. I know just the man to lead Team GB to gold.

Peter Thompson
Sutton, Surrey

SIR – If breakdancing is to be included in the Paris Olympics, other nations will not have a chance when it comes to team Morris dancing. Bring it on.

David Owen
Eldwick, West Yorkshire

What do you think of it so far?

SIR – I draw your attention to the dramatic change in editorial policy at the BBC. They have not blamed Brexit for our dearth of medals at the Winter Olympics.

Julian Shaw
Portsmouth, Hampshire

SIR – There can be no doubt that the greatest highlight of these Winter Olympics is the commentaries provided on the BBC by Ed Leigh and Tim Warwood. Snowboarding is an exciting sport to watch even without words, but the addition of their descriptive superlatives would make even watching growing grass and drying paint totally unmissable.

Dave Wright
London SE20

SIR – I confidently predict that participants, presenters, commentators and observers will all find the Commonwealth Games to be absolutely incredible. Anyone who can come up with an alternative description would really deserve a medal.

Mike Hart
Mannings Heath, West Sussex

Cambridge turns the air blue

SIR – The BBC has been censured after it broadcast footage of a member of the Cambridge rowing team swearing. As a cox for a school rowing team in the 1980s I can vouch that bad language is a common occurrence in the sport.

In my case, as I was selected for my light weight rather than any particular skills, it was usually my crew rather than me doing the swearing.

James Sneath
Eastbourne, East Sussex

No one to match him

SIR – The loss of Shane Warne has finally corrected the misunderstanding as to when the word "spin" should be used. It should only be deployed when discussing cricket and should not be borrowed when describing politicians' actions

The "King of Spin" will always be called Shane, not Peter or Alistair or any other such name that comes to mind.

Jonathon M. M. Baker
Upton Noble, Somerset

SIR – The experiment with picking new, inexperienced "batters" in cricket has clearly failed. We should revert to picking more traditional and experienced "batsmen".

Mark Shaw
Heathfield, East Sussex

SIR – How refreshing to see the word "batsman" in the headline and article on Jonny Bairstow. I think he has certainly proved he is not a Yorkshire pudding.

Phil Vallins
Cambridge

SIR – Stephen Fry refers to the simple "politeness" of using the term "batters". I am regularly asked by my captain to take the position of silly mid on and find the term most offensive. Surely sensible mid on would be more polite.

Roger Evans
Cookham Dean, Berkshire

Dust and ashes

SIR – Not being able to sleep I turned on the radio and heard the words "in, out, in, out" over and over again. Was this a repeat of the Boat Race, or had I perhaps stumbled upon a nocturnal hokey cokey convention?

Regrettably, it was England batting. Surely we can provide sterner opposition than this!

John Deeley
Burton on Trent, Staffordshire

SIR – What a shame that your news item about the proposed replacement of the England men's cricket team with the women's team was only an April Fool's Day joke.

Tim Leete
Burgess Hill, West Sussex

SIR – Anticipating the next Ashes series, it might make for a more equal contest if England had the Australian bowlers in their team and Australia had the English bowlers.

Michael Upton
Nottingham

SIR – The England cricket team poses a threat to the public health of Australia and should be deported. Many Australians are at risk of dying laughing.

Keith J. Vaughan
Great Stretton, Leicestershire

SIR – Having seen the wonderful victory by the England cricket team at Trent Bridge, I was minded to consider how many of those lucky spectators, who were offered free entry, were "working from home" that day.

Christopher Wood
Ashington, West Sussex

SIR – I am delighted to report an excellent standard of cricket was in evidence at this year's Eton vs Harrow match. The chanting was good-natured and amusing, although Eton struggled to respond to the Harrow chant, "Winston Churchill, Boris Johnson".

Paul Simpkin
London SE3

SIR – If only our Government were as good as our cricket team.

Wendy May
Hereford

SIR – Did a rogue blue sock find its way into the washing machine for the England men's cricket kit?

Roger Wilson
Charter Alley, Hampshire

Djokovic courting controversy

SIR – One way to improve our Test team is to put the tennis champion Novak Djokovic in to open the batting. After all, it took the Aussies two weeks to get him out.

Dave Alsop
Churchdown, Gloucestershire

SIR – Following his comments on the Covid-19 vaccination programme, I understand that Novak Djokovic is now to be known as Novax.

Ian Nalder
Nairn, Inverness-shire

SIR – It's not unusual for small boys to be scared of the needle. Novak Djokovic needs a good Scots nanny.

David Tallon
St Albans, Hertfordshire

SIR — As Mr Djokovic would appear to believe there is one law for him, and one for everybody else, I reckon that if he comes here to play Wimbledon, he could join Boris Johnson's Government.

Gordon Pugh
Claygate, Surrey

Advantage ours

SIR — We have just returned from a river cruise in France, with what we considered a typical summer cold. Subsequent Covid testing gave a positive result. My wife is delighted. She no longer needs an excuse to stay in and watch Wimbledon.

Bob Fleming
Leicester

SIR — Now is the time for strawberries and cream, Pimm's and the BBC continually telling me I have to change channels if I want to continue watching this match.

Derek Bennion
Epsom, Surrey

SIR — For next year's Wimbledon tournament I am going to design some headwear for the male competitors. It will be very similar to a baseball cap, but with the peak at the front.

Nairn Lawson
Portbury, Somerset

SIR – Could Rafael Nadal please purchase looser underpants that would enable him to stop fiddling with himself in between each shot.

Jane Bunner
Chipstead, Surrey

SIR – If I had £5 for every time Tim Henman said, "you know", I could keep myself, family and neighbours in Pimm's for the whole of Wimbledon.

Derek Long
Evesham, Worcestershire

SIR – Support for finalists at Wimbledon this year presaged the election for a new prime minister.
    Who to choose when none appeals?

Martin Mayer
Chorley, Lancashire

SIR – Since its foundation in 1877, the men's tournament has been named the gentlemen's singles.
    Has anyone thought to inform Nick Kyrgios?

Judith Rose
Marlow, Buckinghamshire

SIR – My wife of 55 years has started to call me Kyrgios. The trouble is that I am not sure which of his qualities is responsible for this.

Philip Ryder-Davies
Wickham Market, Suffolk

SIR – Nick Kyrgios may "attract a new generation to tennis" according to the BBC. Oh dear. Is that the petulance, the anger, or the obscenities?

Stephen Godber
Newark, Nottinghamshire

Life in the fast lane

SIR – I've always thought Formula One would be far more interesting with half the cars going clockwise round the track, and the rest anti-clockwise.

Rupert Godfrey
Lacock, Wiltshire

SIR – The BBC has been accused of not giving the game of bowls due recognition.

The trouble is that I do not envision a game where the slow-motion replays are faster than the real action ever gripping the audience to the extent of, say, snail racing.

Martin Henry
Good Easter, Essex

What a beautiful game

SIR – I took my wife to Aston Villa (big mistake). When the playing paused, she asked a heavily tattooed gentleman: "How long is the interval?"

When he regained his composure, he said: "You mean half-time, Missus."

Another visit is not on the cards.

Peter J. Robinson
Lichfield, Staffordshire

SIR – It is rumoured that shortly after Ukraine won their World Cup qualifier against Scotland, Kremlin officials, investigating strange noises coming from the president's office, discovered Vladimir Putin on the floor chewing the carpet.

Robert Readman
Bournemouth, Dorset

SIR – Perhaps a job swap between Gareth Southgate and Boris Johnson is the answer. The UK would have a thoughtful, respected prime minister and the England football team might acquire some of the elan and chutzpah apparently needed to succeed at the World Cup.

Alan Honeyman
Scarborough, North Yorkshire

SIR – It was suggested on Woman's Hour that the football team currently enjoying such success should be called the Lions rather than the Lionesses. The proponent of this argument should understand that it is the lionesses which do most of the hunting for the pride, while the males sit at home expecting to be pandered to.

Nick Pope
Woodcote, Oxfordshire

SIR – Good for the Lionesses! Just goes to show: if you want something done, ask a busy woman.

Jacqueline Davies
Woodbridge, Suffolk

SIR – The thing that I like most about women's football is that it is so much more gentlemanly than the men's game.

Jeremy Somers
Chipping Norton, Oxfordshire

It's all kicking off now

SIR – Go on, admit it; there is plenty to be gloomy about but you're all enjoying "Wagatha Christie".

Alisdair Low
Richmond, Surrey

SIR – Coleen Rooney and Rebekah Vardy are much like Ant and Dec, in that nobody knows (or cares) which one is which.

Ray Aldis
Salisbury, Wiltshire

SIR – I assume that Robert Rinder must be busy with other projects, because the best place to hear this childish nonsense would be in the court of Judge Rinder.

Paul Morley
Skipton, North Yorkshire

SIR – Rooney 1 - 0 Vardy. Please let it be the final whistle.

Kirsty Blunt
Sedgeford, Norfolk

SIR – The coverage of the "Wagatha Christie" case should surely be in the entertainment section of the paper.

Nigel Griffiths
London NW4

THAT'S
ENTERTAINMENT

Conditions today will be nonsensical

SIR – The BBC Radio 4 pre-news weather forecast resembles a session of *Just a Minute*.

Trying to determine your area's weather from the gabble is nigh impossible.

Wes Thomas
Truro, Cornwall

SIR – Forecasters have begun to refer to a new point of the compass – the wast.

David Jones
Cambridge

SIR – The only thing missing from the reports on the hot weather is Boris Johnson standing at a lectern, brandishing the slogan, "Stay Home – Drink Water – Protect the NHS".

Bob Britnell
Canterbury, Kent

SIR – In the animated film *Chicken Run*, all the birds wear scarves to disguise the join where their heads are stuck on. Does this explain why, whatever the weather, so many TV presenters also wear them?

John Roberts
Wokingham, Berkshire

We regret to inform you

SIR – I suggest the traditional phrase "The end of the world is nigh" should be replaced by Huw Edwards intoning: "I am now joined by our Health Editor..."

Dr Robert Walker
Workington, Cumbria

SIR – The automatically generated subtitles for the BBC's coverage of the State Opening of Parliament relayed that Black Rod had summoned "members of dishonourable house" to the Lords.

Has the BBC's voice recognition technology become as contemptuous of this current Parliament as the rest of us?

Roy A. C. Ramm
Felsted, Essex

SIR – My thanks to the Government for providing an alternative to live panto with the grandchildren. We can now sit in the comfort of our own home with Today in Parliament.

Jeremy M. D. Moger
Hazelbury Bryan, Dorset

SIR – One of the most unfortunate side-effects of Partygate is that it has somehow given Andrew Neil a vehicle with which to return to our screens.

Mark Robbins
Bruton, Somerset

SIR – What will the BBC do to fill their airtime if Boris does resign or is defenestrated? The gap they will need to fill is gargantuan.

> **Garth Inman**
> Coltishall, Norfolk

SIR – A new definition for the BBC – the Bash Boris Corporation.

> **James Montgomery**
> Bideford, Devon

SIR – Boris Johnson had to go.
   Huw Edwards, the Leader of the Opposition, said so.

> **John Knowles**
> Berkhamsted, Hertfordshire

SIR – Reports of war, natural disasters and murders are never going to be made "enjoyable" for the viewer by a newsreader on a "catwalk".
   Whatever next? Huw Edwards in a miniskirt and stiletto heels?

> **Susan Cawley**
> Arnside, Cumbria

SIR — I assume that broadcasts from the remodelled studio will be along the lines of: "Hi boys and girls, nice bit of news for you today, 21 million are starving to death in Africa at the moment. And here's something else for you to get excited about: North Korea has devised a more efficient bomb and is hoping to try it out on the Isle of Wight soon.

But you won't like the next bit, England cricket…"

Michael Turner
Winchester, Hampshire

SIR — I thought about staying up for the news tonight but realised that "Vladimir isn't a decent chap, and nor is Boris" just about covers it.

Julia Sharpe
Salisbury, Wiltshire

SIR — Is there anyone employed by the BBC who is NOT going to the Eurovision Song Contest?

Andrew Boddey
Stourport-on-Severn, Worcestershire

Reporting under fire

SIR — Note to broadcasters; the Ukrainian capital is pronounced Keyev, not Keef, which makes it sound like a member of the Rolling Stones.

Andy Holmes
Bromley, Kent

SIR — I would like to reassure everyone that we are not heading, as some reporters would have it, for a nucular war. If it happens it will be a nuclear one.

Stephen Saunders
Hindhead, Surrey

SIR — Seeing Clive Myrie reporting from the hotel rooftop in Kyiv, I was disappointed that when the air raid sirens sounded he didn't say, "I've started, so I'll finish."

Roger Gullen
Walkern, Hertfordshire

SIR — Having just watched the BBC's excellent programme on Thatcher and Reagan, I believe it should be compulsory viewing for Joe Biden and every European leader. Also Putin, although I don't think he would enjoy it.

Peter Flesher
Halifax, West Yorkshire

SIR — Should anyone be seeking light relief in these sombre times, I recommend a visit to the RT (formerly Russia Today) television channel.

As its reporters and presenters strain with increasing desperation to spin the news in Moscow's favour, they are becoming "a source of innocent merriment".

Rather than ban the channel, as the EU has done, I think the Government should positively encourage us to dip into its output from time to time.

John Carter
Shortlands, Kent

What's on the menu

SIR – The BBC primetime schedule for 19 May reads as follows:
BBC One 8pm *Eat Well For Less*
9pm *Gordon Ramsay's Future Food Stars*
BBC Two 7pm *Rick Stein's Secret France*
8pm *Britain's Top Takeaways*.
One could be forgiven for feeling a little satiated.

Linda Johnson
West Lavington, Wiltshire

SIR – Thanks to Covid-19, I have lost my sense of taste. I now have a sudden urge to watch *Love Island*.

T. Tavernor
Tarporley, Cheshire

SIR – It's pretty clear we have now moved from kitchen sink dramas to large kitchen island unit dramas.

James Logan
Portstewart, Co Londonderry

SIR – What has happened to Pop Larkin's farm? Is it still there or is it now a housing estate?

> **Dr Steven R. Hopkins**
> Scunthorpe, Lincolnshire

SIR– I'm coming out; I'm prepared to admit I am an avid *Neighbours* viewer.

> **Michael Cattell**
> Chester

SIR – I am glad that *Neighbours* has come to an end. I hold it responsible for the unfortunate, widespread adoption of the irritating Antipodean inflection?

> **Jane Brown**
> Caterham, Surrey

SIR – I hope that *Only Fools and Horses* carries a Trigger warning.

> **Catherine Nield**
> Via email

SIR – Watching a BBC Two programme titled *How to Sleep Well* with Michael Mosley, I demonstrated its effectiveness by falling asleep before the end.

> **Bruce Denness**
> Niton, Isle of Wight

SIR – How kind and ingenious of the BBC, amid all our troubles and woes, to create a simple diversion for the viewer. It is called *The Antiques Roadshow* and, as far as I can gather, the viewer has the almost impossible task of discovering the antique amid the Elton John hats, the autographs of The Beatles, Barbie dolls, jewellery from the 1970s and jolly uncomfortable but garish chairs of the mid-century.

J. P. Chilcott-Monk
Winchester, Hampshire

SIR – I can take anything this or any other government throws at me, but Jeremy Paxman presenting *University Challenge* without a tie may be a step too far.

John Potts
Bognor Regis, West Sussex

SIR – TV programme title of the year must go to the BBC's *Pointless Celebrities*.

Richard Finch
Ravenglass, Cumbria

SIR – Boris Johnson doesn't know who Lorraine Kelly is. Good news at last; he has my full support.

Edward Christian
Wiveliscombe, Somerset

Uneasy listening

SIR – When I was young, The Archers was "An everyday story of country folk".

Heaven help the country folk today.

> **Lise Lavery**
> Nutbourne, West Sussex

SIR – As a nine-year-old boy I listened to the first episode of The Archers with deep and lasting disappointment. I'd thought it was going to be about Robin Hood.

> **Colin Bostock-Smith**
> Uckfield, East Sussex

SIR – I have decided that, after death, we either go to heaven, or listen to the idiotic presenter of BBC Radio 3 early on Saturday mornings.

> **Trevor Wye**
> Salisbury, Wiltshire

And the show goes on

SIR – Somewhere, Humph clears his throat.

"Hello, and welcome to the newest series of *I'm Sorry I Haven't a Clue*. On my left, Willie Rushton and Tim Brooke-Taylor. On your left, Jeremy Hardy – and please welcome back Barry Cryer."

Rapturous applause.

> **Steve Cattell**
> Grantham, Lincolnshire

SIR – I am sure that Barry Cryer would have been delighted to have been featured on the same obituaries page as Sir Crispin Tickell, and would soon have had him arriving at the *I'm Sorry I Haven't a Clue* ball with daughter Tess.

Tim Barnsley
London SW16

SIR – Although Bernard Cribbins was most famous for *The Railway Children*, I first enjoyed his novelty songs such as "Right Said Fred" in 1962. For the last 60 years his voice and warm smile have always been around, and I thought that he was immortal. I couldn't have dreamed of a better tribute than that from Matthew Sweet in *The Daily Telegraph*: "It's like being told that chocolate digestives have been discontinued."

Dave Alsop
Churchdown, Gloucestershire

SIR – With Lester Piggott, Terry Wogan and Margaret Thatcher now all gone, is life worth living?

Brian Lawrence
Witham, Essex

Will Smith's new hit

SIR – "...and the Oscar goes to Will Smith for his tearful apology."

Susan Sang
Petersfield, Hampshire

SIR – One luvvie slaps another luvvie at an absurd ceremony. Doubtless they are talking of little else on the streets of Kyiv.

> **Huw Baumgartner**
> Bridell, Pembrokeshire

SIR – The Academy Awards clearly needed to attract more viewers, but that was probably the wrong way to go about it.

> **Emilie McRae**
> Trowbridge, Wiltshire

SIR – Will Smith for President.

> **Michael Jones**
> Burnley, Lancashire

THE RIGHT ROYALS

Sussex, USA

SIR – You have started printing pictures of the Duke and Duchess of Sussex again.

Please stop.

Jeremy Nicholas
Great Bardfield, Essex

SIR – Prince Harry is quoted as saying we should all imagine being a "raindrop". I wonder if he has been talking to Yoko Ono.

William Havercroft
Oxford

SIR – Prince Harry wants employers to give staff 45 minutes of "inner time".

We used to call that "lunch time".

Peter Calver
Knebworth, Hertfordshire

SIR – Just when I thought I would never laugh again, the Sussexes win the NAACP President's Award for public service.

Bill Galvin
Stockport, Cheshire

Andrew high and dry

SIR – Prince Andrew is apparently giving millions to somebody whom he has never met.

I'm going to join the queue outside Buckingham Palace.

Graham White
Cambridge

SIR — Anna Pasternak wonders how the Duke of York will fill his time. Here are a few suggestions. The interiors of several Royal residences could do with a lick of paint, if the interior photograph in the article is anything to go by. There must be plenty of lawns to mow and flower beds to weed.

Like so many of those made unwillingly redundant in recent years, he's sure to find plenty of unpaid work. If desperate, he could take out an annual subscription to Ancestry, for which I can provide a half-price code, though I suspect his discoveries won't be as exciting as those of the common user. If he finds himself in need of cash, he could apply for one of the millions of job vacancies around the country. Fruit picking in autumn, for instance?

Mary Ross
Warrington, Cheshire

SIR — If the Queen wants to scupper the future of the monarchy, by all means let the Duke of York back on board and sink the ship.

John Watson
Oban, Argyll and Bute

SIR – Andrew should find a rock far, far away, crawl under it and never show his face again.

David Tucker
Stokenchurch, Buckinghamshire

Long live the Queen

SIR – The Queen is turning 96, and not surprisingly people of this great age find it very difficult to walk. I rather like the idea of Her Majesty processing down the aisle of Westminster Abbey in a mobility scooter, with everyone on either side bowing or curtsying as she zooms past.

Simon Toynbee
Rolvenden, Kent

SIR – A memorable morning at school in the 1950s. The teacher entered and said: "I have two important things to say. First, I have lost my pen and secondly, the King has died."

Strange priorities, but perhaps it was an expensive fountain pen.

Barbara Solomons
London NW4

SIR – I am embarrassed to admit the headmaster's announcement of the King's death, to my assembled prep school, generated barely suppressed whispers of "new stamps".

Freddie Spicer
Dorchester

SIR – When George VI died I was very warm, secure and comfortable, but had no particular thoughts about the event because I was three weeks away from being born.

> **Mary Alexander**
> Tunbridge Wells, Kent

SIR – Spurred on by the Women's Institute's corgi-knitting initiative for the Jubilee, my wife has sharpened her knitting needles, reviewed stock of available wool, mailed regret notices to numerous social and charitable invitations, and battened down for the duration. I am, of course, retained as a consultant.

> **Roger Fowle**
> Chipping Campden, Gloucestershire

SIR – I have just received an email advertisement for a Jubilee hot tub.

I had no idea merchandising had spread its tentacles so wide. I hope it has been appropriately endorsed.

> **Tim Hadland**
> Duston, Northamptonshire

SIR – Both the Archbishop of Canterbury and Prince Andrew must have been bitterly disappointed that Covid prevented them from attending the Queen's Platinum Jubilee celebrations. The Lord works in mysterious ways.

Philip Fawkes
Lyndhurst, Hampshire

SIR – The Queen's Platinum Jubilee celebrations will be remembered for the number of female guests who decided to wear a satellite dish at a jaunty angle on their heads. It is just as well there was little wind as there could have been deadly frisbee-type objects flying everywhere.

Brian Christley
Abergele, Conwy

SIR – In the wake of Her Majesty's balcony appearance over the Jubilee weekend, I found myself musing on the question of how the three heirs might carry forward her successful concept of "I must be seen to be believed". Lime, pastel blue, yellow and fuschia are not readily available in men's suits. Nor are coordinated hats.

Eleanor Patrick
Elsdon, Northumberland

SIR – Having observed the performance of the military during the Jubilee celebrations, I wonder whether it could be invited to take over the management of the Civil Service.

Ken Jones
Hambledon, Hampshire

SIR – Let us hope that Putin has watched the celebrations surrounding the Platinum Jubilee and has learnt something of what a good, nay great, head of state actually looks like.

Robert Pugh
Llandeilo, Carmarthenshire

SIR – Important anniversaries in some countries are marked by the aggressive goose-stepping of robotic soldiers, while terrifying modern machines of destruction are paraded through the streets.
But in Britain we see normal people march with dignity in historic costumes, while others follow behind doing imaginatively daft things to the obvious delight of the monarch and the whole country.

We are rightly proud, but don't take ourselves too seriously.

Where would you rather live?

John Gordon
Datchworth, Hertfordshire

SIR – Alongside all of our dear Queen's many laudable and admirable attributes, let us not forget that she remains our most glamorous Bond girl.

Jeff Snowden
Bardsey, West Yorkshire

If you go down in the woods

SIR – Following the release of weekend video footage from Buckingham Palace, news from Nutwood is that Rupert Bear is questioning claims that Paddington is the nation's favourite bear.

Peter H. York
Daventry, Northamptonshire

SIR – The sketch featuring the Queen and Paddington Bear caused me to laugh out loud from start to finish. By far the best comedy I have seen on TV for years. And British to its core. A Bafta for Her Majesty?

Keith Allum
Christchurch, Dorset

SIR – I wonder how many Jubilee street parties were changed at the last minute to include marmalade sandwiches.

David Pearson
Cambridge

SIR – Surely, now that we know what Her Majesty keeps in her handbag, it should hereafter be called "ma'amalade".

> **Mary Sutherland**
> London SE10

SIR – At the Queen's first Jubilee in 1977 I was asked to go to a street party dressed as Paddington Bear. The children recognised me but the fathers did not. Suddenly one of them bit me on the back of my knee very hard and went around the party saying, "I bit the bear", causing great mirth and then a whole queue of other fathers wanting to do the same. Paddington fled.

> **Click Mitchell**
> Tetbury, Gloucestershire

SIR – After the Queen, it would appear that Paddington Bear was the star of the Jubilee. I fear, however, he was eclipsed during the pageant by a bravura performance from Basil Brush on an open-top bus. When can we look forward to seeing him back on our screens?

> **Gary Spalton**
> Liskeard, Cornwall

SIR — Although the marmalade sandwich sensibly stored in Her Majesty's handbag "for later" has provoked much interest, the true star of the vignette before the Jubilee concert was the vast, hideous and splendid red tea cosy.

This will undoubtedly become the Christmas gift of choice this year, so I suggest that the souvenir shop opposite the Palace begins stitching immediately to satisfy demand.

Alison Gallico
Morpeth, Northumberland

USE AND ABUSE
OF LANGUAGE

I beg your pardon?

SIR – Using the word "common" (along with saying "pardon", or "toilet") was considered dreadfully common when I grew up in the 1950s.

Even using it in this letter made me die a little.

Felicie Oakes
Birmingham

SIR – I must take issue with your claim that US officials under the administration of George W. Bush would have ever described Mr Lavrov, Russia's foreign minister, as "a complete a---hole". Clearly they would have used the American "a--hole" rather than the English "a---hole".

Toby St Leger
Oldmeldrum, Aberdeenshire

SIR – I am SHOCKED to read the offensive Latin word *cacor* in your report on graffiti unearthed at Vindolanda in Northumberland.

Further and alternatively I am OFFENDED that you bowdlerise its translation into "s---ter".

Is it perhaps a matter of concern that my valet might notice the article while ironing my newspaper? Sadly in these days of reduced households the task falls to my butler, who regularly spars in classical languages with Jeeves at the Junior Ganymede.

Stephen L. Phillips
Chirk, Denbighshire

SIR – In response to the announcement of an exorbitant fee increase "per anum" (sic), a literate parent at the school at which I was teaching confirmed that he would prefer to pay through the nose as usual.

Roger Potter
Sherborne, Dorset

None the wiser

SIR – Today I saw a van on which was printed a three-consonant company logo, and the phrase "Specialists in so much more than just the obvious". Is this the least informative tagline ever?

Dr Mark Betteney
London SE9

SIR – I was bemused to discover we have an organisation called Natural England, but I was mightily impressed to see that it has a "Director of People and Nature". I can't even control my ball on the golf course.

Martin Prentice
Tunbridge Wells, Kent

SIR – Jacob Rees-Mogg writes, "It is helpful of David Frost to call for a bill to sunset EU law."

As Calvin and Hobbes put it, "Verbing weirds language".

Michael Rogers
Sevenoaks, Kent

SIR – A few years ago before undergoing a minor hospital procedure, I was antibioticated.

Bob Farey
Kettering, Northamptonshire

SIR – If so many people no longer know what a noun, verb, adverb or adjective are because they are no longer taught this in school, how will they know what words should not be used to finish a sentence with?

Brian Smith
Dunfermline, Fife

Lost in translation

SIR – Following the recommendation by the Information Commissioner's Office that Latin words and phrases should not be used in public life, as so few people understand them, I trust that the "Exit" signs will be removed from all public buildings.

Philip Goddard
London SE19

SIR – The English language is going down a pitiful cul de sac.
But *nil desperandum.*
Chacun à son goût.
And we don't all have to join them.

Diana Gibbons
Pulborough, West Sussex

SIR – A Cambridge antiques dealer once told me
how a historian friend of his had been invited to give
a public lecture in Japan. It would be accompanied
by a simultaneous translation. The speaker was not
required to submit a script in advance, but told his
translator that he might include a joke which could
be omitted if it proved too tricky. "Don't worry," the
man said, "I'll know what to do." The lecture was a
triumph, and at the critical moment the audience
duly fell about laughing. The speaker congratulated
the translator afterwards and asked how he had done
it. "Oh, it was just too difficult," said the man, "so
instead I said only, 'Here the professor makes a joke'."

Robert Grant
Cambridge

SIR – An Anglo–French conference on fishing rights
in the Channel was equipped with simultaneous
translation delivered through headphones. The
French decided that a particularly knotty point could
only be settled by discussion with the local fishermen.
Their spokesman said, "We will have to leave this to *la
sagesse Normande*." This was translated as, "We will have
to leave this to Norman Wisdom."

The French were baffled by the hysterical laughter
from the British.

John Crooks
London SW15

Ill feelings

SIR – With calls to rename monkeypox "hMPXV", amid concerns that the current name could stoke racism and stigmatisation, what is the future for other common diseases? German measles denigrates an entire nation, chickenpox might offend poultry farmers (and be confused with "bird flu"), smallpox is sizeist and meningitis is clearly sexist.

> **Michael Bacon**
> Bordon, Hampshire

SIR – One benefit of the pandemic has been that people now understand that "data" is a plural noun. If only we could achieve the same for "bacteria" and "criteria".

> **Antony Dew**
> London SW13

SIR – Why "face masks"?
  I await hand gloves and feet socks.

> **Guy Bargery**
> Edinburgh

You don't have to be mad to work here...

SIR – Civil servants have been told to say "absurd" rather than "crazy" in case the latter stigmatises the mentally unwell. I would like to suggest that such a ruling is barking, but suppose that it would be offensive to dogs.

Charles Smith-Jones
Landrake, Cornwall

SIR – I had hoped to construct an ornate stone patio in my garden. However, despite an exhaustive trawl through Yellow Pages, I have been unable to secure the services of an absurd-paving contractor.

Terry J. Neale
St Mary, Jersey

SIR – I wonder how many absurd people are employed by the Treasury.

On the evidence, more than a few – especially in HR.

Perhaps this can help to explain our present economic predicament.

Tim Instone
Bath, Somerset

SIR – My dictionary appears to be out of date. Would you please publish the 2022 meaning of the words "civil" and "servant"?

Gillian Lurie
Westgate-on-Sea, Kent

Striking phrases

SIR – It is time to banish the Orwellian term "industrial action". It means the opposite of what it states: inaction.

John Jones
London SW19

SIR – I think to describe things with the prefix "smart" – e.g. motorways, phones, meters – is to offer excellent examples of oxymorons. A bit like "fun run".

Tony Greenham
Sutton, Cheshire

SIR – If the Watergate building had been called the Waterprat, subsequent events might have been more entertaining.

Tim Hadland
Northampton

SIR — I quite like the "-gate" suffix. I'm waiting for a certain billionaire to steal the door to someone's garden so we can have Gatesgategate.

Rory Mulvihill
Naburn, North Yorkshire

SIR — Our election candidates evidently now run for office. That is what they have always done in America, but I thought that we were more restrained and stood for office.

Chris Cleland
Farnham, Surrey

SIR — Collective noun for a lack of policies: a Starmer.

Andrew Siddons
Walsall, Staffordshire

SIR — It should be a matter of considerable regret that the item most evident in the legacy of the three wasted years under Theresa May is her bequeathing us the quasi-tautological "deliver on".

Dermot Elworthy
Tiverton, Devon

SIR – I doubt if Boris Johnson's successor will have quite the gift he has for inventing wonderful words, as in his description of Sir Keir Starmer as "Captain Crasheroony Snoozefest". It inspired me to have a go. The best I could come up with was a word meaning to attempt to seize the moral high ground on issues such as racism with the intention of using it to undermine an opponent – "jiggery-wokery".

Martin Smith
Barnet, Hertfordshire

SIR – I have invented a new word for the English language. My word is "sarcastafob".

"Sarcastafob" means sarcastically fobbing you off while remaining achingly polite. I have invented this word to describe how Chichester District Council communicates with me via email. However, I suspect that there are many others in this country who may feel "sarcastafob" accurately describes how their own councils talk to them.

Kevin Mann
Bosham, West Sussex

Putin his place

SIR – The French spelling of Putin is "Poutine", pronounced "Pouteen".

This is, no doubt, to ensure that it does not rhyme with "*putain*", a colourful word whose meaning and usage will be known to anyone familiar with the language of Molière.

I know which pronunciation I prefer.

> **Terence Morrison**
> Castledermot, Co Kildare, Ireland

SIR — Instead of footling about on whether to call it Chicken Kiev or Chicken Kyiv, it would send a stronger message to call it Chicken Ukraine.

> **Sandy Pratt**
> Storrington, West Sussex

SIR — Hopefully the appropriation of the letter "Z" by Putin's gang of thugs will make that letter a pariah, finally leading America to spell "apologize" etc. correctly.

> **Finlay Mason**
> Luxembourg, Belgium

SIR — I have removed the zed from my scrabble game.

> **Robert Ward**
> Loughborough, Leicestershire

Playing up a storm

SIR — We will shortly experience Storm Eunice, as nice and gentle a name as one could conjure. Get real: let's follow Eunice with Storm Flippineck, followed by (if naming then returns in fashion) Storm Gordon Bennett.

> **Roger Fowle**
> Chipping Campden, Gloucestershire

SIR — Is there any way I can prevent my name from being used to identify a storm or other form of bad weather incident? I imagine there must be a very disgruntled Eunice Dudley somewhere in the country.

Allan Muirhead
Kirkby Lonsdale, Cumbria

SIR — Eunice is a fine, strong name. It originates from two ancient Greek words: *eu*, meaning good, and *nike*, meaning victory and equivalent to, but stronger than, the English name Victoria, which originates from the Latin noun for victory.

Were I to meet an old maid called Eunice, I would definitely be on amber alert at the very least.

Claire Bourne
Dorchester, Dorset

Man/woman/other

SIR — Having recently seen the demises of FireMAN, PoliceMAN and ChairMAN, I wonder if I should be worried.

Tony PalfraMAN
Disley, Cheshire

SIR — A chair is an item to sit on. Is this how most board and committee members view their leaders?

Susanne Burton
Wedmore, Somerset

SIR – Halifax has introduced pronoun badges for staff.

Here in deepest Lancashire the bank's reputation could have risen had it insisted that all staff be referred to by the usual "luv", "duck" or "sweetheart".

Eric Kirkby
Bolton, Lancashire

SIR – My own badge has worked well for many years. It reads SIR.

Bob Pawsey
Hungerford, West Berkshire

SIR (OR MADAM) – Should I add other possibilities?

Dr Jeff Haggett
Brighton, East Sussex

SIR – Would it be too selfish of me to select me/me/me for my nametag pronouns?

David Evans
Ashbourne, Derbyshire

SIR – I'm not sure exchanging the terms "miss" or "sir" for "teacher" would always work. Sometimes when absorbed in a task, a pupil of mine would call me "mum".

Pat Banton
Burton on Trent, Staffordshire

SIR – I stop referring to ladies as girls when they are over 70. They then become old girls. I am 79 and am an old lad.

Tom Gibson
Stockport, Cheshire

SIR – There is an obvious solution to the problem of how to address each other. Give everyone a doctorate. It's the logical progression of grade inflation.

(Dr) R. Allan Reese
Dorchester

SIR – Recent political discussions regarding gender identity have often referred to the word "penis", which I find rather grating. I suggest "picnic attachment" instead.

Edward Leigh-Pemberton
Faringdon, Oxfordshire

The long and the short of it

SIR – I'd like to start a society called the Drop out of Society Society. Unfortunately this would be shortened to Dross, but since that's how we are treated normally then there would be no offence taken.

Caroline John
Alton, Hampshire

SIR — I see that the Government's bill to revitalise the country's planning system is based on the principles of Beauty, Infrastructure, Democracy, Environment and Neighbourhoods which provide the rather unfortunate acronym of BIDEN — a name hardly synonymous with invigoration and progress.

Robert Stranks
Horsham, West Sussex

SIR — As wives and girlfriends of footballers are termed "Wags", why not "Pops" for partners of politicians?

Hyder Ali Pirwany
Okehampton, Devon

SIR — A "wag", as defined by Dr Johnson, was "Any one ludicrously mischievous; a merry droll". In the late 18th century it was a voguish word, so much so that Charles Dibdin (1745–1814), best known for his ballad "Tom Bowling", wrote an entertainment (a one-man musical show for singer/actor and piano) entitled *The Wags or The Camp of Pleasure*. It ran for 108 performances when it opened on 18 October 1790.

Jeremy Nicholas
Great Bardfield, Essex

Just saying

SIR – The first time I said "Fine words butter no parsnips" to my husband, he had never heard it before, and thought I was giving him a shopping list.

Beverly Cox
East Knoyle, Wiltshire

SIR – Have readers noticed how life has become so much easier since discussions became conversations, and difficulties were transformed into challenges?

Trevor Wye
Salisbury, Wiltshire

DEAR
DAILY TELEGRAPH

Serious business

SIR – Please request that Alex is properly dressed. He would never discard his tie.

Robin Knight
London W4

SIR – After checking every word, paragraph and story in the 1 April edition of *The Daily Telegraph*, I reckon there are three April Fool stories and at least three maybes.
  Comments, please.

Eddie Peart
Rotherham, South Yorkshire

Problem solved

SIR – Having *The Daily Telegraph* in two sections is a great bonus, and makes for a much calmer breakfast table. If you could put the puzzle page in the Features section as well, I am sure the divorce rate would drop even lower.

Amanda Baly
Saxmundham, Suffolk

SIR – Having finally managed to free myself from
the addiction of doing the Wordle puzzle every day,
I am distraught that you have added PlusWord to the
puzzles section. I just hope my willpower is strong
enough to avoid being dragged back into that world.

Richard Sinnerton
Woking, Surrey

SIR – I've had an Eric Morecambe moment while
playing today's Wordle. On my third attempt I got all
the right letters, but not necessarily in the right order.

Stephen Gledhill
Evesham, Worcestershire

And now we go to our reporter

SIR – Douglas Murray was making much of "schtick"
in his article on Saturday, but I am a sad person who
has no idea what a "schtick" is.

Is it something I schould throw for my schpaniel to
chasche after?

Yoursch,

Andrew H. N. Gray
Edinburgh

SIR – I note today's front-page headline announcing: "Pestering women on the street to be outlawed". I am sure that there are many men out there unwillingly dragged into Christmas shopping who would heartily agree with this proposal.

Derek Bedson
Harlech, Gwynedd

SIR – You report on a pilot study to use drones to deliver medicines to the Isle of Wight. Surely this is a no-pilot study.

David Oliver
Langley, Berkshire

SIR – The first sentence of your report on 28 February states, "Soldiers have called for vegan uniforms to be introduced across the Army to fall in line with dietary requirements."
    Thank God I was in the RAF – we never, ever had to eat our uniforms!

Alexander Simpson
Market Drayton, Shropshire

SIR – Am I the only one who had to read the headline "Public count of walruses from space to be verified" a couple of times?

Neil Bunyan
Bedford

SIR — The Queen's Platinum Jubilee has given us all cause to rejoice. It was an especial honour, as Swordbearer of London, to be on the steps of St Paul's Cathedral as members of the Royal Family arrived for the Service of Thanksgiving.

However, my highlight of these Jubilee celebrations has been Tim Stanley's description of me, in his article on 4 June, as "a boy in an enormous fur hat". As I am old enough to have been around during the Silver Jubilee, such a flattering depiction is a reason to rejoice indeed.

> **Tim Rolph**
> Swordbearer of London Mansion House
> London EC4

SIR — In the late 1960s a regular sight along Oxford Street was the sandwich-board man declaring: "Repent! The End is Nigh!"

Was that Allister Heath's father by any chance?

> **Patrick Kelly**
> Chippenham, Wiltshire

SIR – My coffee was cold, there was only a scrape of peanut butter left, my daughter and grandson were heading for the (frozen?) North and my son and family might or might not make it here from Belfast. My wife has something nasty on her shin which is to be probed this afternoon and my damn prostate is playing up (again). But thank God for Allison Pearson – I laughed and laughed over my scantily covered toast.

Tom Ridout
Salisbury, Wiltshire

The people have spoken

SIR – In the expectation of having a letter published, I wish to complain about coronavirus, the NHS, Tony Blair, Boris Johnson, Russia and China, energy costs and indeed about everything. I won't even start about the cricket.

David Nunn
Port Isaac, Cornwall

SIR – In the last few days there have been several letters from Lincolnshire. Sir, you are in danger of putting us on the map.

Elizabeth Bellamy
Cleethorpes, Lincolnshire

SIR – At last, you have published another letter from Roger Gentry. I thought something might have happened to him.

Andrew Howison
Walton Highway, Norfolk

SIR – *I'd like to get a letter printed in the* Telegraph,
I write amusing poems that would make your readers laugh,
I do not have a title or impressive rank (retired),
But my grammar and my spelling reach the standard that's required.

To say that you're elitist would be untrue and unkind,
And the word misogynistic hadn't even crossed my mind,
But ordinary folk need more expression in the press,
They've got a lot of common-sense opinions to express.

The mess that is our Government has caused the same despair
As to the Lords and Colonels, and we've grievances to air,
On all the usual suspects I'd like to have my say,
So I hope you'll print this letter in the Telegraph *TODAY!*

Liz Machacek BSc Biology Teacher (retired)
Housewife (they don't)
Penn Bottom, Buckinghamshire